Out of Control

Out of Control

Why Disciplining Your Child Doesn't Work—and What Will

Shefali Tsabary, PhD

namaste
PUBLISHING

Vancouver, Canada

ABOUT THE EXAMPLES IN THIS BOOK
Although the examples in this book reflect real-life situations, they aren't necessarily descriptions of actual people, but in some cases are composites created from my years of working with countless different parents in many varied contexts.

LIBRARY AND ARCHIVES CANADA
CATALOGUING IN PUBLICATION

Library and Archives Canada Cataloguing in Publication

Tsabary, Shefali, 1972-, author
    Out of control : why disciplining your child doesn't work-- and what will / Shefali Tsabary, PhD.

ISBN 978-1-897238-76-9 (pbk.)

    1. Discipline of children. 2. Child rearing. 3. Parent and child. I. Title.

HQ770.4.T72 2013   649'.64   C2013-904560-0

Published in Canada by
NAMASTE PUBLISHING
P.O. Box 62084
Vancouver, British Columbia, V6J 4A3
www.namastepublishing.com

Distributed in North America by PGW, Berkeley, CA USA
Typesetting by Steve Amarillo, Urban Design LLC
Back cover author photo by Laura Rose

Printed and bound in Canada by Friesens

people and it's time we stop! Here's the book that will guide us toward doing it differently—with more consciousness, connection, and love.

— CARRIE CONTEY, author of
    CALMS: A Guide To Soothing Your Baby

Out of Control will transform your relationship with your children by helping you become the parent you always dreamed you could be. Dr. Shefali's wonderful book is bursting with practical wisdom, and we enthusiastically recommend it to all parents!

— BARBARA NICHOLSON and LYSA PARKER, cofounders of Attachment Parenting International and co-authors of *Attached at the Heart*

A powerful book to help families transform their relationships forever. This book goes straight to the heart of the problems we share with our children and gives us a clear path to turn them into powerful lessons.

— AMY MCCREADY, founder, Positive Parenting Solutions & author of *If I Have to Tell You One More Time*

Dr. Shefali's provocative book title does not disappoint. With passion, compassion, and wisdom gained from her own parenting mistakes and her clinical research and experiences, she skillfully reveals why authoritarian parenting styles, controlling our children, and punishing disobedience don't achieve the goals or relationship we desire with our kids. And even better, she shows us what does!

> — KEITH ZAFREN, founder, The Great Dads Project
> and author of *How to Be a Great Dad—*
> *No Matter What Kind of Father You Had*

Dr. Shefali has done it again—expanded the parenting lens all the way to the core—and this time, with a focus on how we discipline our children and why. As with her last book *The Conscious Parent,* the traditional parent- child relationship is flipped on its head so that we, as parents, can see with new eyes. *Out of Control* offers distinct guideposts that can be used to untether ourselves from outmoded ways of controlling our children. Dr. Shefali always gives a clear and deep invitation to elevate our parenting to new heights, and this new book is no different. The reader will never see discipline in the same light again, allowing a true soul-to-soul rather than role-to-role relationship to bloom and awaken wholeness within both the parent and the child. I highly recommend Dr. Shefali's rich and textured offering on what it truly means to be an effective parent.

> — ANNIE BURNSIDE, award-winning author
> of *Soul to Soul Parenting*

Refreshing, challenging, and life-changing! This book takes a deep and long look at our role as parents and what it truly means to teach our children self-discipline, authenticity, and empowerment. It takes a daring parent who takes the first steps towards conscious engagement. This book will usher you on this journey with wisdom: sometimes a gentle prod, and at other times a big push. Either way, you will end up taking a giant leap forward!

> — LORI PETRO, speaker, parent-educator & founder, TEACH through Love

Profound and trail-blazing, this book sets itself apart by creating an entirely new approach to child discipline. Dr. Shefali brilliantly and instantly makes this complicated topic accessible, offering parents clear, useful, and invaluable guidance. This book is a gift to our children, and to those who care deeply about their future and their potential.

> — JESSE A. METZGER, PhD, clinical psychologist

Rarely does a book come along that can shift you from your core and catapult you into a new way of thinking, feeling and behaving. *Out of Control* is such a book! It goes to the heart of why it is we have conflicts with children and challenges us to engage with children from a new place entirely—a much more evolved, free, and joyous place.

> — JULIE KLEINHANS, education transformation expert, certified coach, teacher and mentor for parents and youth

Out of Control is a superb book on society's greatest task—nurturing, raising, and honoring its children. Dr. Shefali expertly dismantles our oldest crutch, that of discipline, and provides us with concrete instructions on how we can help our sons and daughters become happy, healthy, confident, and self-regulating. Amazingly, she does it without preaching! A must-read for parents and educators.

> — SAIRA RAO, president, In This Together Media

This book is a game-changer. It turns the entire notion of discipline on its head and shows us a new way—a revolutionary way that achieves results. If you want your children and your relationship with your children to evolve and flourish, this book is a must-read!

> — BELINDA ANDERSON, certified life coach & author
> of *Living from the Inside Out*

A brilliantly written, insightful, and refreshing parenting book! *Out of Control* invites parents to shift from the archaic crime and punishment approach to bad behavior, to a new paradigm that shows them how they can consistently harness the power of natural consequences to raise their children to become more responsible, empathic, and resilient.

> — DAVINA KOTULSKI, PhD, author and psychologist

Dr. Shefali leaves no stone unturned in her mission to change our perspectives on parenting. She dares to challenge the cultural paradigms that have become primitive and are counterproductive to creating the positive experiences we wish for our children. After reading this book, every parent will begin the quest of honest self-reflection, insight, and ultimately change. This is the greatest gift we can give our children: our own growth.

— MICHAEL MATALUNI, host of Kick Ass Dad /
Passionate Parenting In A Volatile World

Dr. Shefali teaches us that it is through first embracing our true selves that we can then connect with and celebrate the true self of our child. Through that connection we enter the most precious "space between" of vulnerability, curiosity, empathy, and attunement. Traditional discipline in its many forms inhibits that connection. Dr. Shefali's book articulates a new way of approaching problematic behaviors and impasses that frees us to deepen the connection with our children and heal their pain and our own.

— SUSAN NORTHRUP ELDREDGE, LCSW,
psychotherapist

Dr. Shefali has hit it on the nail yet again. She once again shows us how parenting is really *all* about us. By revealing our darkest anxieties, she shows us how we pollute our children's development instead of enhancing it. This is a must-read for every parent who wishes to evolve their parenting to another level. It has irrevocably altered the way I think in and outside of my parenting role.

— BEVERLEY ANDERSON, autism specialist

If only I had read *Out of Control* in my early years as a parent and teacher. Little did I know that I was using methods of discipline that were actually working against me! This book clearly lays out why it is we enter dysfunctional patterns with our children and what we need to do to prevent these. This book has completely changed the way I teach and parent. I wish for every parent and teacher to undergo the transformation it has gifted me.

— MALINI HORIUCHI, NYC teacher and parent

Reading Dr. Shefali's brilliant book *Out of Control* can be painful, in the same way it can be to stare at a hated facial quirk in the mirror for too long. You may recognize some ugly truths about yourself and your parenting. But through vivid anecdotes and wise insights, Dr. Shefali reshapes those ugly truths into beacons of light. By the end of the book, you'll feel armed with the knowledge and strength to break the cycle of control and begin a new era of parenting, to both your own and your children's benefit. Tough but fair, blunt yet beautifully written, *Out of Control* is a must-read for any parent who feels uncomfortable with how they handle discipline and is in need of guidance.

— SUZANNE COBB, editor, *Kids in the House*

Out of Control is a brilliant and powerful book! The insights and wisdom inside these pages will absolutely transform every parent's relationship with their children for the better. As a mother of a 13- and 12-year-old, I have experienced first-hand how parenting with discipline fails time and again, but have been at a loss for alternatives. Dr. Shefali offers them here, and they are sheer excellence. Every parent should read this book!!!

— STEPHANIE GUILBAUD, mother of two

Dr. Shefali's new book *Out of Control* is the parenting book we've all been waiting for. Her book dives deep into the importance of conscious parenting and why outdated methods of punishment and discipline are ineffective and often damaging. This book offers a new paradigm, a way to view the parent-child dynamic through a present-day lens rather than through past experiences and future worries. This allows an authentic relationship to develop—a relationship based on mutual respect and understanding rather than fear and blame. Parents who utilize this book will undoubtedly experience more compassion and empathy for themselves, and their children.

— CATHY CASSANI ADAMS, LCSW, CPC, author of The *Self-Aware Parent* and host of Zen Parenting Radio

Dr. Shefali's book is transformational on every level. She shows us how we can connect to our children beyond their surface behaviors and reach their core, heart, and essence. And isn't this what every parent ultimately wants? As a trained behavioral therapist, this book was at first a challenge to my ways of thinking. However, once I looked past my own comfort zone, I was able to see its jewels and reframe some of my own views within the parent- child dynamic.

— Ferzin Patel, M.A., behavioral therapist

We need to listen to our children, hear what they are saying, and let them be who they are. Dr. Shefali's new book *Out of Control* shows us how. She reminds us that discipline is not guidance and that thoughtful guidance is what our children need. A must read for all parents and all parents-to-be.

— Karen Frigenti, principal of The Summit School, NYC

Dr. Shefali beautifully explains how our relationship with our children, and our children's behavior, starts with us. While other books tell parents how to manage kids, this one tells parents how to change and understand themselves first. A must read for any parent or caregiver.

— Sean Eckenrod, author, *Allie Gator and the Seven Stones* and blogger at www.Respect4kids.com

Be done with the naughty stool and the time out corner! There is a new approach in town—one that will revolutionize the way you parent your children forever. Dr. Shefali shows us how we can engage with our children in a deep and authentic manner, without relying on artificial techniques and quick-fix strategies. This book is a must-read for anyone who wishes to empower, inspire, and motivate their children.

— TANYA PETERS, PhD, clinical psychologist

If you only read one parenting book this year, make it *Out of Control!* The title says it all! Our kids, and even us as parents, are Out of Control, and it's time to learn how to shift. Dr. Shefali's gentle, powerful, and effective approach to parenting is refreshing. In a world where parents either let children rule the roost with disastrous lifelong effects, or where parents are stuck in the "because I say so" mentality that raises followers, not leaders or happy people, she teaches us how to find the saner path. This book is packed with great, easy-to-apply tips, and written by a parent who just happens to be a psychologist, as well.

— JACQUELINE GREEN, host of the Great Parenting show

Preface

Rarely does a book come along that breaks with the way society tends to do things and challenges us to a new approach entirely—especially when it hits us literally "right at home."

For many, if not most, the content of *Out of Control* will be something strikingly new. For some it will be experienced as a *shock*, akin to a physical whiplash or a whack on the head. For others it will be confirmation of the way they are already parenting, providing them with the insight and support they simply can't find in most places.

For many like myself who have adult children, the question that will spring to mind is, "Where was this book when I was parenting?"

The simple fact is that we were unaware of the amazing insights Dr. Shefali Tsabary shares with us in *Out of Control*. Though we loved our children and did the best we could, our methods were based on the kind of parenting we experienced in our own upbringing. Consequently, we didn't really know to rear our children differently—in a more gentle and validating way that would result in their being self-assured, happy, and responsible adults.

Words from a song from the sound track of *Jesus Christ Super Star* come to mind: "May we start again, please?" And the good news is, "Yes!" As parents, and anyone involved in childcare.

When we look at the way societies have functioned for a very long time now, we find that much of what has been traditionally accepted as "how things are done" no longer serves us in this era of increased freedom, privilege, and awareness. The deep cracks in society's institutions as a result of the earthshaking changes we are experiencing are evident everywhere—not least in our families and our children.

Up until now, we have lived in a predominately patriarchal society, which is reflected in the structures and operating methods of all our major institutions.

This "power over" model has worked because, until recently, most of us have bought into the idea that without *enforced* obedience—control—everything would simply fall apart and there would be chaos.

We are in the midst of a significant shift from a world built on power *over* others to a world in which there is universal equality and mutual respect. So, of course, this is going to hit us right were we live and breathe daily: our family life, and more specifically how we relate to our children as their parents.

Dr. Shefali invites us, even implores us, to advance from the conditioned patterning of relating to our children from a position of parental "power over," to honoring our children by endeavoring to use this sacred relationship to connect with that which is most precious in them and us. In order to do this, invariably we will have to address our own wounded upbringing so we can be healed by parenting our children from a higher sense of awareness.

Let us brave the opportunity of growing up our children, while at the same time being open to letting them grow us up—of being their most loving stewards in such a way they develop the self-sufficiency to scale the highest moral mountain and cross the most forbidding rapids of life with confidence and success. They come to us not from our own seed but from that of the divine. We have the opportunity and honor to be their ongoing gardener—to water, weed, fertilize, appreciate, and hold with gratitude until the plant is sturdy.

Most of us are familiar with the saying, "They shall be known by their fruits." Well, using a similar metaphor, "We as parents will be known by the garden we grow."

Okay, I have just heard my Editorial Director saying, "Enough already. Don't give away the book!"

Constance Kellough
Publisher, Namaste Publishing

Contents

Dedication

To my daughter Maia.

*It is from mothering you that I have learned
to discipline my own undisciplined ego
and evolve into a more humane adult.*

*Your ability to know, honor, and validate
yourself astounds and enlightens me daily.*

Acknowledgments

Constance Kellough—your trust, belief, and support have been invaluable. Without your vision, none of this would have come to fruition. With the utmost gratitude.

David Robert Ord—your partnership and editorial genius have been the backbone of this book. Your presence in my life is one of my most cherished gifts.

To all the clients who have allowed me to enter their lives—your courage to seek change is inspirational.

My family—you are my greatest blessing, my psychic landscape, my emotional foundation. Our relationship means the world to me.

My daughter Maia—I can only aspire to a smidgeon of your inherent self-ownership and empowerment. You are my teacher bar none.

My husband Oz—you saw what I couldn't and you kept believing when I gave up. You are my rock; our relationship is my fire.

Chapter 1

Why Discipline Doesn't Work

"My child just doesn't listen to me," a parent tells me. "No matter what I say, I may as well be talking to the wall. Homework is a nightmare, chores are a constant battle, everything is a struggle."

"What did you do the last time you were caught up in a struggle?" I ask.

"First I yelled at her. Then I threatened to take away some of her privileges."

"Give me an example."

"Instead of doing her homework, she was playing games on her computer all evening long. So I took her phone away for two weeks."

"What happened then?"

"All hell broke lose. She yelled at me, saying she hated me and never wanted to talk to me again. She wasted another two hours crying in her room. I'm running out of things to take away from her. Nothing makes a difference!"

Does this sound familiar?

Which parent hasn't threatened their children at some point? If they are mouthy with us, we take away television time. If they roll their eyes, we cancel their play date. If they don't do well on an exam, we deny them a trip we promised them to Disney World. If they don't clean their room, we take away their iPod. Caught in a cycle of *If you don't_____, then I will_____*, we exhaust ourselves trying to control our children.

Most parents find themselves in an endless system of bartering with their children. I call it the "prisoner-warden" approach to parenting, in which the warden is required to closely monitor the child's actions. The child, in the role of prisoner, does something right or wrong. The parent, acting the part of the warden, swoops in to dish out either a reward or a punishment. The prisoner soon becomes dependent on the warden's control to regulate their behavior.

This system of rewards and punishments undercuts the child's capacity to learn self-discipline, subverting their inherent potential for self-regulation. Becoming a mere puppet whose performance is entirely dependent on the warden, the child learns to be externally motivated rather than internally directed. As the years pass, it becomes unclear who the warden is and who the prisoner is, as both torment each other in endless cycles of manipulation.

It isn't a happy situation for any parent to be in the role of warden. I ask parents if they like this role, to which they vehemently answer, "Absolutely not." Yet when I point out how they are in fact playing this role and suggest they stop, they look at me as if I had two heads.

I say to them, "Disciplining your child by taking away their phone, or by yelling, grounding, or slapping them, only perpetuates the problem instead of resolving it. You are seeing the evidence right before your eyes that *discipline doesn't work.* If it did, your child wouldn't still be engaging in this behavior."

Is there anyone who doesn't believe we have to discipline our children? I believed in discipline for years. I yelled, tried time outs, and threatened. I believed it was what was required of me as a parent. No wonder then that when I suggest to parents that discipline isn't only unnecessary, but actually feeds the negative behavior they are trying to correct, it's as if I had asked them to give up a birthright.

When we engage with our children from the belief that child discipline is a vital aspect of our role as parents, we assume children are inherently undisciplined and need to be civilized.

"What do you mean?" parents demand indignantly. "How can I not discipline my child? They won't do anything if I don't scare them or punish them." Hearing the almost panicked tone of these parents, I realize how entrenched most of us are in our belief that discipline is a cornerstone of parenting. I also see the repercussions of this approach to parenting, in that the child truly won't do anything without being threatened or bribed because they have become addicted to being constantly controlled.

When we engage with our children from the belief that child discipline is a vital aspect of our role as parents, we assume children are inherently undisciplined and need to be civilized. Ironically, the most heavily disciplined children are often those least able to control *themselves*.

Without ever really thinking it through, we've bought

into the belief that without discipline, children run wild. We interpret all their misbehavior through this lens. I'm suggesting just the opposite. What we think of as "discipline" is detrimental and fails to produce the kind of behavior parents so long for in their children.

Originally the word "discipline" had a benign meaning, associated with education and training. But ask any parent today about discipline and they assume you are talking about a strategy to control a child's behavior—a strategy that revolves around the parent exerting their will over the child.

Parents actually ponder the question, "What can I take away from my child that my child particularly enjoys, so they'll get the message?" It doesn't occur to them to ask whether the thing being taken away is in any way related to the behavior. The parent believes that depriving their child of this particularly treasured item or privilege will jolt the child into paying attention.

To see how nonsensical this approach is, let's translate it to an adult level. After you have agreed to go on a diet, your spouse catches you cheating with a bag of donuts, and takes away your car keys to prevent you going to the donut shop again. Now, how do you feel? Or you are late for a lunch date with a friend, so your friend demands you give her your favorite piece of jewelry. Again, how do you feel?

I think we can agree that such actions are counterproductive to developing a good marriage or a strong friendship, let alone to keeping you away from donuts or being tardy again. Well, much of what we call "discipline" is just as nonsensical to our children—and just as deeply resented.

Ask yourself, what's the connection between:

If you lose weight, we can go to Universal Studios

If you make the swim team, you can have a sleepover with your friends

If you get an A grade, you can go with grandma to the movie

If you don't do your homework right now, I am not buying you new shoes

If you don't speak to me politely, I'll take away your phone

If you don't stop lying to me, you will be grounded for three weeks.

Parents admit to me, "I find myself making threats without even thinking about it. I feel so angry, they just fly out of my mouth. Then once I make them, I have to follow through, or my child will think I don't mean what I say—and then all hell will break loose."

I respond, "Maybe things improve for the moment. But by using this approach, has the situation been permanently changed?"

Every parent of whom I ask this question admits, "No, never." As one person confided, "I hit that wall when my oldest was four. I thought, 'It can't have to be this way. Human beings, kids, are good!' She is now eleven, and she has never seen, nor heard, nor experienced blackmail, threats, or punishment." The fact is, this heavy-handed, dominance-based approach achieves nothing positive. Indeed, research has verified that punitive techniques carry long-lasting detrimental consequences.

Whenever I talk about this a parent will say to me, "But I was disciplined. In fact, my father walloped the life out of me—and I turned out fine."

I don't get into a debate about whether the parent is truly "fine." I've learned that such a debate fails to get to the heart of the matter. Instead I ask, "How did you *feel* when you were being punished or beaten as a child?"

If the parent is honest, they then say something like: I hated it, I cried a lot, It terrified me, I hated myself, I just wanted to run away.

I ask the parent, "So why do you discipline?"

Predictably the answer is, "Because I want my children to learn. How will they learn if I don't teach them?"

If our aim is to teach a child, I've already hinted that discipline is the *enemy* of teaching. Contrary to what almost everyone believes, far from being synonymous, discipline and teaching are worlds apart.

To illustrate this, think back to how you felt when you were sent to your room, your favorite television program was turned off, you were grounded so you couldn't see your friends, your phone was taken from you, you were yelled at, or you were spanked. Did you feel good? Did it become natural for you to do what it intended to teach you? No, what you learned is, "My parents are the boss, so don't piss them off." You likely also learned that your parents treat other adults, work associates, and maybe even pets with more respect than you.

Because discipline seems related to their parent's whims rather than something reasonable, it always triggers resentment in children. Though they may comply with our demands because we force them to do so, internally they develop a resistance not only to what we are asking of them, but even more so to us as the messenger. Their resistance, or at best half-heartedness, intensifies the parental need to control, as the parent bears down on the child, believing the stricter they are the more the child will comply. It's this resistance that becomes emotional plaque, creating barriers to learning, growth, and—most of all—connection between the parent and child.

The child's behavior may fall in line, but their heart doesn't. There's no buy-in on our children's part.

Chapter 2

A World that Majors in Control

The mother was having an epic meltdown, the worst it had ever gotten. Words slung, feet stomped, doors banged. She felt like screaming. Or running away. Why couldn't her daughter just do as she was *told?* The child was impossible.

It was always the same—toys left out everywhere. Hadn't she told her daughter to pick them up an hour ago, and several times since? But *still* it wasn't done—and their dinner guests were arriving in only fifteen minutes. With so much to do in the kitchen, and now on top of everything the living room to tidy, the mother was about to lose her mind. Snatching up toys and angrily tossing them in the toy box she yelled, "You bad girl! Why don't you ever listen? Why do you always have to be so difficult?"

The four-year-old watched her mother flail her arms and make scary faces. She saw her bang things and talk like she was really, really mad. She heard big words: "responsibility," "punishment," "discipline." What did they mean? She didn't know. She was just plain scared. So scared that she felt like peeing right there on the spot. But that would make Mommy even angrier, so she kept talking to the urge in her head: "Pee pee don't. Pee pee stay. One, two, three."

When would Mommy become happy Mommy again? When would the clouds go away? The little girl hated when the clouds came. They always seemed to come lately—and it was all her fault.

Do you see yourself in this mother? I see myself because the mother was me, and my daughter was the child.

Or was it that *I* was the child?

Mix together a busy schedule, a daughter whose agenda was different from my own, guests about to arrive, coupled with a need on my part to control everything, and all it took was one more thing to set me off. I would blow, venting at my daughter, blaming her for the stress I was feeling. If she chose to be defiant, all bets were off. After all, wasn't it my right as a parent to discipline her, even my duty?

Much as I told myself my daughter "deserved" to be punished, I knew my reaction to toys all over the floor was out of proportion and had more to do with my need to control than with her actions. So I felt bad for exploding at her and promised myself I wouldn't get so angry with her again. Until the next time she did something to set me off, that is, and then I couldn't help myself.

Again and again, if my child appeared out of my control, *I* went out of control. I would feel my chest becoming tight, my throat constricted, my jaw clenched, as in seconds I morphed from a kind mommy into a raging tyrant.

Before I became a parent, I would never have thought myself capable of such outbursts. One minute infuriated, the next nauseated by the way I had inflicted so much pain on my child, I was confounded by my anger.

As a psychologist and therapist I find that, like me, my clients tend to become hooked on control. If anything goes wrong or we are pushed just a little too far, we lose our balance. Of course, afterward we're always sorry and perhaps downright embarrassed by our anger, power plays, and guilt tripping. Yet when our children don't do what we need them to do, we don't know any other way to spur them to action. It's like getting your emotions caught in a blender with no control over the speed dial.

When I experienced a loss of control in this way, it was as if I'd taken a time capsule back to my own childhood. I was suddenly four years old again, stomping my feet, pitching a fit, desperate to get my way. The reason I was triggered in such an intense way with my daughter is that the present situation was reawakening emotions from my past. I have vivid memories of occasions in my own childhood when guests were coming to dinner and my mother was in a state of total panic. Even though I resented how controlling she became at such times, I internalized her feelings. Lurking just beneath the surface of my civilized veneer, these emotions now sprang to life with my own daughter, subverting my sanity and hijacking all reason.

The patterns of behavior we witness in childhood become the template for our own way of parenting. How our parents made us feel lingers in us unresolved, becoming the lens through which we interpret our children's behavior. In other words, much of how we interact with our children is governed by what's often referred to as our "subconscious."

To some degree we are all slaves to our past, and our children have a way of bringing this out. It's because, even if the precise events that imprinted us appear forgotten, they still drive us at a subconscious level until we face them and resolve the emotions surrounding them. It's no wonder that, in my practice as a therapist, I frequently encounter men and women in their forties, fifties, and sixties who are still emotionally trapped in childhood, unable to escape the echo of their parents' rage, put-downs, neglect, and control.

The patterns of behavior we witness in childhood become the template for our own way of parenting.

Every conflict in our present lives—whether with our children, spouse, or other adults—is in some way a recreation of our childhood. Every relationship, every interaction is based on a blueprint from our own upbringing. In one sense, then, there are no adults in the room; we are all just children acting out. When it comes to parenting, we are in many ways *children raising children.*

Janet is an example of what I'm describing. Things became so bad between her and her ten-year-old son that, every time he entered the room, she found herself tensing up, dreading the conflict she knew was almost certain to follow. Tracing this feeling back in therapy, she realized she was experiencing the same helplessness she used to feel around her father, who regularly beat her. All these years later, her son's "all boy" boisterous energy, which was at times quite aggressive, was triggering her unresolved past.

Without realizing it, Janet was reacting to her son as if he were her father, which is why she was immediately on the defensive around him. Their almost daily fights only served to cement her belief that her son was a tyrant—an image of males that had more to do with her father than with her son. In other words, a pattern of behavior established decades ago with her own parents was now in the driver's seat when it came to how she parented.

Children who are dominated grow up either to dominate or be dominated. This is why for generations a belief in the parent's right to dominate and control has prevailed—especially a father's right to "decide" for the family, a phenomenon often referred to as "patriarchy."

As one client in her forties related, "When I was a young girl, my mother would sometimes say, 'Your father is Lord and Master of the house.' My brother and I believed her. My father's angry look ensured compliance with the way he said things should be. A child's smooth cheek needn't be struck many times for the message to get through. Even my father's clenched jaw became enough to bring me into line. Another favorite maxim in our home was the familiar 'children should be seen and not heard.' For me, the parent-child relationship was clear: obey or else. My preference in any situation wasn't on anyone's radar screen, including my own. In retrospect, I can see I've lived most of my life unaware I had a choice in anything. Blaming someone or something 'out there' became as reflexive as breathing."

Generations the world over have subscribed to an approach to parenting which states that, by reason of age and experience, the parent is at the top of a pyramid and the child by default at the bottom. The idea is that children should fit into the parent's world, not the other way around.

I often hear people say, "They are my children, and I'll decide what's good for them." Many believe that, because we brought our children into the world, we own them. It's as if they were one of our possessions. This mistaken notion feeds our belief that we have a right to dictate to them. Based on this flawed idea, we justify coercion, manipulation, and even physical punishment. Of course, we couch it as "teaching" and create a philosophy called punitive "discipline," coming up with fancy strategies, techniques, and gimmicks. Volumes are written on the subject. Yet if we are courageous enough to admit it, all forms of "discipline" are just temper tantrums in disguise. Did you ever think of much of what we call "discipline" as nothing more than an adult child pitching a fit?

Unless we realize the entire premise of heavy-handed punitive discipline is based on our delusion of superiority over our children, the daily struggles with behavior that play out in our homes, in the classroom, on the playground, and in the conflicts of the wider world will continue unabated. Indeed, this authoritarian approach to parenting is largely responsible for the world as we know it—whether we are talking about a woman in midlife who has never followed her own voice because her father insisted he was "in charge," dictatorships that tyrannize their subjects, or nations that seek to subjugate other nations in international conflict. The root of the dysfunction we experience as individuals, nations, and a world lies in the belief that people need to be controlled—a belief that, no matter which culture or part of the world we come from, pervades our parenting. The need to dominate is what discipline is all about, and this domination is responsible for much of the emotional distress that has characterized our species for eons.

If you look at most of the supposedly "great" men of the past, they were in many cases tyrants who sought to conquer. Their "greatness" was achieved through control, at the expense of those they subjugated. Whether we are talking about individuals such as Alexander the Great or Napoleon, or empires such as Rome or the British Empire, they were driven by a need to dominate and control.

Just as most of the world evaluates "greatness" in terms of how much control a leader achieves, so too "good" citizens—like "good" children—are those who comply. And who are the most compliant of all citizens? Aren't they the military, which functions entirely on orders and prizes discipline above all else? Uniform behavior is the gold standard in a world that majors in discipline.

In contrast, once in a while a leader arises on the world scene who dramatically improves the wellbeing of other humans. Though such leaders have been few and far between during the course of history, who of us wouldn't want our child to grow up to be a truly good leader—maybe even a great leader who fosters peace, prosperity, and wellbeing? Who of us doesn't want our child to grow up to be a freethinker, a trailblazer, original and innovative? Who of us doesn't want our child to be true to who they really are instead of docile, easily manipulated, and controlled by others?

We say we want these things for our children, yet our addiction to discipline sabotages the very goals we set for them. A diet of control, compliance, and conformity guarantees either mediocrity and an acceptance of the mundane, or dictatorship and tyranny.

Some parts of our world have in many ways moved beyond the Dark Ages, through the Renaissance, and into a more enlightened era. We don't put people in the stocks anymore, don't burn them at the stake because they have different religious beliefs from us, and for the most part don't believe that sickness is a punishment from God. Ours is a far less hierarchical, more democratic era than has existed on the planet until now.

Though there is an increasing awareness of the importance of valuing human beings and treating them fairly, together with a growing consciousness of the importance of caring for the planet, when it comes to raising our children most of us are sadly still stuck in the Dark Ages. Through being disciplined, children the world over are daily discriminated against, often horrifically and with tragic results.

It's therefore time to change the entire paradigm of parenting, at the core of which is the flawed idea of authoritarian discipline—that is, "lording it over" our children heavy handedly, instead of working with them in a constructive manner that encourages them to become self-disciplined.

Chapter 3

Is It Really for Your Child's "Own Good"?

"As I sit here and think of all the times I felt crushed by my parents," a client said to me, "I can't believe that at 41, after all the years of work I've done to move past the anger, sadness, and disappointment over how I was treated, just thinking about it can still cause a great big lump in my throat and bring tears to my eyes. No matter how old I get, no matter how wise I become, I still can't wrap my brain around how a grown man can take a small child no more than two years old and lock her in a dark, dank, cement closet in the basement, tell her the bugs are going to get her for being naughty, and leave her there for who knows how long. He let me scream, kick at the door, and yank on the door handle. His only response to my terror was the sound of his footsteps fading as he ascended the steps."

This father undoubtedly deluded himself into believing he was teaching his child a valuable lesson. No doubt he imagined that by instilling fear in his daughter, he could pull her in line. He had bought into the theory that parents need to use heavy-handed control strategies if they are to be effective.

Explaining their rationale for even the most bizarre forms of discipline, parents often tell me, "I'm doing this for my child's good." They are surprised when I point out that no child ever feels that being yelled at, grounded, or spanked "is good for me." For them, the only takeaway from such an interaction is resentment. Over time this resentment can grow into a bitter self-loathing that can turn their life to chaos as a cloud of low self-esteem descends, attracting people and situations that mirror the way the individual thinks of themselves.

So blinded can we parents become, so wrapped up in our ideals, that we cause immense damage to our children. If we believe something is for our child's own good, we may go to any extreme to force our ways on them. Just how damaging this can be is evident in an incident in which a mother was jailed for a minimum of seventeen years because she beat her seven-year-old son to death, then set fire to his body. The judge explained that it was the child's "failure to learn" passages of a holy book that had been assigned to him "that resulted in the beating that caused his death." Speaking directly to the mother, he continued, "...you had kept him home from school so he could devote himself to his study," which involved "memorizing passages." The judge added, "The cause of the beating was your unreasonable view that he wasn't learning passages quickly enough." How many other children have been beaten because they failed to learn something either at home or in school?

The seven-year-old's mother clearly held a subconscious agenda that caused her to believe it was necessary to beat him if he was to learn. By "agenda," I mean what's really going on beneath our surface actions and statements. Her attachment to an idealized image of herself as a good mother who taught her son her faith caused her to lose touch with the reality of his age, capacity for memorization, and perhaps interest.

Terrorizing a child is a terrible thing to do—unless you want to teach them to terrorize. We would never do such things, we assure ourselves. Yet we don't realize that even the seemingly benign ways in which we seek to control our children are counterproductive.

There's a new wave of discipline in town that goes under the names of "gentle" discipline or "conscious" discipline. These are an oxymoron. Sure, they have a clear intent to do no physical harm, but they are often heavily masked strategies for inducing the same conformity as traditional discipline, just in less aggressive ways. Such discipline has the effect of weakening the child's inherent desire to self-regulate.

No matter how good our intentions may be, any kind of discipline leaves our children feeling attacked. They hate being disciplined, not because they resent doing the right thing, but because threats, arm-twisting, and punishment belittle them. They sense we are trying to control them, and their naturally free spirit feels helpless—like someone who is locked up for a crime they didn't do. Whenever we ground them or in some other way discipline them, they can't help but want to defy us all the more in order to preserve some semblance of self-respect. The more we attack them, the more quickly "I hate being grounded" becomes "I hate you, I hate my life, I hate myself."

To discipline is actually painful for many parents. Mothers especially somehow intuit that heavy-handed discipline such as spanking their children has a deleterious effect. This is why in many cases they leave it to the father. The problem is that parents don't know what else to do. They are often at their wits' end, which easily leads to losing it with their children.

Little wonder that the first thing parents say to me in workshops is, "Give me some strategies to get my child to listen to me. How can I get them to obey? The approach I'm using isn't working. Help me."

It's great that the parent is asking questions, though the questions don't quite get to the heart of the issue. It isn't a question of how to discipline, but of understanding our children's needs. A child's behavior is just the expression of their needs, which fall into two categories: connection and learning. Correction is fundamentally different from connection. Correction is sadly associated mostly with punishment—witness the way we call prisons "correctional institutions."

Because we have been trained to read only a child's behavior and not what's behind it, we get sucked into the superficial level of the child's actions. For example, a child says, "I hate you!" The parent takes the statement at face value, making it a personal issue, which calls forth a reprimand. If instead the parent looks deeper, uncovering the reasons for the child's outburst, they may discover that the child is being bullied at school, is anxious about an upcoming exam, or is upset as a result of being unjustly punished earlier in the day. It's also possible the child is simply tired or hungry.

Instead of reacting emotionally, the parent needs to calmly decipher the meaning behind the behavior and shift from the content of the child's eruption. The key is that the parent remain centered, not thrown off balance by the remark, so they can gently probe for the real issue.

The role of a parent is to help a child learn for themselves. But who can learn when they are consumed by defensiveness, if not resentment and even outright hatred? The last thing a child who feels this way wants to do is learn. All they can think about is getting back at their parents—or getting far away from them.

In other words, *discipline results in acting out.* How the child has come to feel about themselves is now projected outwardly in dysfunctional behavior. In this way discipline becomes the root of what parents see as rebellion.

Discipline simply misses the mark. The issue isn't whether to discipline or how to discipline, but whether we are really engaging with our children. Sadly, in my clinical experience, few parents know how to engage. Many parents actually feel isolated by their children, shut out of their world—especially when their child enters the teens, as the years of being disengaged finally come to a head.

Eventually the message our children get when we threaten, bribe, or punish isn't that we care about them or are interested in what they are learning. With their natural self-respect eroded by our continual attacks on their integrity, the message they get is, "I must be so bad that I deserve to be punished." This then translates to feelings of self-hatred, self-doubt, shame, and guilt—again, hardly the conditions for learning.

When our children are given the message that their behavior is more important than their feelings, it's as if we are telling them, "What you feel doesn't matter, and therefore you don't really matter. All that matters is how you make me look." As a result of our focus on behavior instead of feelings, disconnection begins.

The crucial point I want to make is that our connection with our children always happens at the feeling level. We think it's about behavior, when it's really about the way a child feels in our presence.

> It's because discipline focuses on behavior, not on the feelings driving the behavior, that it undercuts the very thing we are trying to accomplish.

If we aren't connected to their feelings, we will never be able to connect in terms of their behavior. Imagine seeing your child heavily engaged in some type of play or craft or drawing or whatever they love to do. That look of concentration and focus. Do they look like that when they are disciplined? It's because discipline focuses on behavior, not on the feelings driving the behavior, that it undercuts the very thing we are trying to accomplish.

If discipline is counterproductive, then how do children best learn? They learn only when they feel connected to us, which fosters calm acceptance and open receptivity. If they are hurt, scared, angry, or resentful, such feelings block their natural inclination to learn. Then we end up constantly harping on themes such as pick up your toys, clean your room, do your homework.

Do *any* of us really enjoy being disciplined? Whether in our personal lives or at the corporate level, don't all of us dread being called into question by an authority? Think of how you feel, for example, if you are unlucky enough to receive a letter informing you the IRS is going to audit you. Why do we dread the auditor's arrival, even if we have paid our fair share meticulously? We dread it because we know that the energy an auditor comes with is fault finding and accusatory. An auditor will try to find things wrong when there's nothing to be found.

Don't those of us who work outside the home hate it when our boss calls us to the office for a "disciplinary" meeting? We know what it's about, and we dread it. At that moment, are we thinking about how we can grow as a person, learn how to do things better, advance in the company? No, all we conjure up are excuses to protect ourselves. After we have been "disciplined," we leave the office feeling embarrassed, if not humiliated. Chances are we don't rush to our desk to celebrate our dedication to the company but wallow for a time in a feeling of having been misunderstood, treated unfairly, and needing to keep our head down. Little does the boss know that our love of our work has diminished—that the disciplinary action generated a feeling of bitterness, so that we end up wishing we could just "find another job where they value me."

When parents approach parenting with the attitude that their child needs to be disciplined if they are to learn, the child feels not only controlled but in many cases inept. This is because discipline inevitably highlights, and thereby reinforces, any weaknesses a child may have. In this way we inadvertently become accomplices in creating the very behavior we then end up punishing.

Chapter 4

Let Consequences Do Their Job

"If I can't bribe or punish them, how do I get my kid to do what I want?" a parent asks. "Surely there have to be consequences for their misbehavior?"

"Indeed there have to be consequences," I explain. "In fact, consequences are precisely how a child learns to be self-directed and responsible. But let's be clear what we mean by 'consequences.' They are fundamentally different from punishment."

A child says to me, "If I don't listen to my mom, I'm going to get a consequence." When I ask what kind of consequence, they tell me something like, "I'm not going to be allowed to go on my play date."

I ask, "So did something happen in the last play date that made your mom decide you may not be allowed to go on another?"

The child replies, "No, the play date was fun. But my mom said I wasn't listening to her."

We may have changed the terms we use, talking about

"consequences" instead of "punishment," but this mom is still punishing her child. She appears to have no clue what it means to *allow consequences to enlighten the child*. Only when a child feels the consequence of their behavior do they get the message. If we impose a penalty, they don't get the message—they simply resent us. The difference in these two approaches is the key to how a child becomes self-disciplined.

We can't just change terminology and expect a different result. The methodology has to change. We can call it "discipline," or we can call it "consequences," but if it's still punitive, then it's just punishment by a more benign name—and our children aren't fooled. Punishment now called "consequences" is still punishment, and the child knows this.

If you are one of those parents for whom the word "punishment" has become a dirty word, it's likely you subscribe to the idea of "consequences." I can't help but smile when a client says to me, "What consequence should I give my child for this behavior?" The particular issue may involve not doing homework, refusing to eat certain foods, not wanting to go to sleep, being sassy, or any number of behaviors. I ask, "What do you mean, 'give' your child a consequence?"

The idea of "giving" consequences misses the point. We don't give consequences. They aren't something we have to pick, as if we were wandering through the aisles of a supermarket selecting items to put in our cart. A consequence is something that's *automatically* built into a situation without us having to "do" anything at all. The moment we imagine we have to "give" our child a consequence, which requires us to think of one, we have moved into the realm of punishment.

Consequences are natural, which means they are directly

connected to the situation at hand. You might say they are inbuilt. All that's required of the parent is to allow the consequence to take effect—and that's the difficult part. We've been so schooled to impose "lessons" on our children that it feels counterintuitive to allow the lesson to emerge naturally out of the situation.

Moving away from discipline requires us to learn how to allow natural consequences to correct a child's behavior. Whereas discipline is counterproductive, exposing a child to the consequences of their actions is a powerful way for a child to learn for themselves.

There are natural consequences to all behavior—positive or negative results that either improve the quality of our everyday lives or make life more difficult. To allow natural consequences to take their course is in no way punitive, but simply a necessary part of helping a child grow up.

Consequences involve no coercion, no bending of our children to our will. Our focus is always on helping our children respond to the consequences of their actions by developing better life skills out of their own resourcefulness, aided by our encouragement and guidance. This approach to parenting requires great discernment on the part of the parent— something that doesn't always come easily, yet is a vital aspect of effective parenting. The parent has to learn to step back and allow life to be the teacher.

> We've been so schooled to impose "lessons" on our children that it feels counterintuitive to allow the lesson to emerge naturally out of the situation.

Consequences are about cause and effect. Most parents believe they are teaching their children about cause and effect, whereas they are doing anything but. Cause and effect is one of the fundamental laws of the universe. It suggests that all actions are interdependent, each caused by something and setting in motion something else. The only reason children don't learn to be self-disciplined is because there hasn't been an effective enough pairing of cause and effect. The most common reason for this is the interference of the parent.

To illustrate what I mean, when we pour too much water into a cup, we cause the effect of spilling. This teaches us not to pour as much water into the cup next time. We touch a hot stove and the effect is we get burned. This teaches us to be careful not to touch a hot stove. We are inattentive while driving, resulting in an accident. This teaches us to pay attention when we are at the wheel. No matter how frequently someone may have pointed these dangers out to us, often we only really "get it" when we experience them for ourselves.

One example of the ways in which we short-circuit the effect of consequences is that, in our desire to protect our children from spilling water, we instruct them each time they get a glass of water not to fill the glass to the top. Consequences are something children naturally learn from, provided the parent doesn't save the child from the effect. When we stay out of the picture, children automatically develop self-discipline, self-reliance, and a sense of responsibility.

The *only* time we should interfere with a natural consequence taking effect is if there is real danger, such as when a child is about to run out into a busy road, swallow a poisonous substance, or in some other way harm themselves or another person. In other words, there are consequences that are inherently detrimental for children on a universal basis that the child may not know about or understand. In these circumstances, the parent steps in.

Other than in such situations, the rule is be careful how you meddle. This doesn't remove a parent's need to prepare their child for life's consequences in the best way they can. Parents have a right to forewarn, helping their child realize that there can be negative consequences to their actions. However, if the child still refuses to take the parent's advice, it's important for the parent to step back and allow the natural consequences to do their work.

The parent's challenge is to be patient, since consequences don't always teach a lesson instantly. Sometimes life has to up the ante before a child learns. For instance, a child may spill water several times when learning to fill a glass. If they have to mop up the spill each time, they learn to be more careful—assuming, of course, they are old enough to have developed the motor skills and muscle coordination required for pouring water into a glass. In the case of a hot stove, one child may touch the stove and never do so again, whereas another child may touch the stove three or four times before they learn. As long as the parent doesn't intervene to save the child from the consequence, providing of course it doesn't involve injury or death, the child will learn. This is because life naturally helps us improve the way we function.

With many of my clients, I find that parents have a hard time understanding the difference between natural consequences, which are the effects of the child's actions, and artificial impositions that go under the name of "consequences." To spell out the difference, let's take the case of a child who doesn't do their homework and is denied their favorite television program. Is this a natural consequence of the child's behavior or an arbitrarily imposed punishment? Well, ask yourself, does the child say to the parent, "Wow, Mom and Dad, I really learned something from this. I'll never do that again!" Or does the child begin to deeply resent the parent, seeing the parent as someone who spoils their fun? The real solution here is neither to punish the child nor protect the child through, for example, excessive tutoring, but to expose the child to the effect of their own lack of motivation. This may take the form of getting a poor grade, which allows the child to experience their failure to respond to their inherent desire to achieve—a feeling that's quite different from resenting a need for achievement imposed on them by the parent.

If a child is rude, they may be told they can't go to their friend's birthday party at the skating rink. If a child hits someone, they often receive a slap from the parent "to teach them not to hit." If a child comes home with a C grade, their cell phone may be taken from them. If a child lies, the computer might get shut down for the next week. These aren't consequences but punishment. They are unrelated to the child's actions and wouldn't naturally occur unless we imposed them. (I'll tell you what is related in the next chapter—but don't you dare skip ahead! There will be a "consequence.")

Artificial consequences don't work because they don't make sense to the child. The child can't connect with them because they are illogical and arbitrarily imposed. I tell parents that unless a consequence truly is a consequence and not a punishment, it will always backfire and thereby perpetuate bad behavior—and in addition cause a rift between the parent and child.

I said that parents inflict "consequences" arbitrarily. I use the word "arbitrarily" intentionally, because "consequences" that are imposed by the parent may involve television privileges, the computer, a cell phone, going to a party, grounding, or a spanking, depending entirely on the parent's mood at the moment. The so-called "consequence" might be severe one day, minimal the next. This isn't a *consequence* at all. Natural consequences are always consistent: touch a hot stove and you get burned.

Whenever something is imposed instead of organic, it will never work in the long run. Artificial "consequences" don't teach the child about real life since the consequences aren't those of real life but are instead idiosyncratically determined by the parent.

Following the natural way allows our children to learn that every action evokes a reaction. Taking ourselves out of the equation and letting them experience the results of their behavior helps them develop a meaningful relationship with their world. Because we are no longer in the middle, between them and their experiences, they don't view us as an enemy to be resisted but as an ally to be sought for comfort, encouragement, and guidance.

Chapter 5

How Rescuing Our Children Teaches Irresponsibility

Why do we resort to arbitrary impositions as a teaching tool instead of allowing the natural consequences of a situation to do their work?

The reason is quite simply that we feel helpless in the face of being unable to control how our child's life will turn out. The feeling of helplessness triggers anxiety. This causes us to resort to overpowering the child's autonomy in the mistaken belief that if we direct their life, the outcome will be more certain. In other words, exercising hierarchical control over a child is an attempt to remove the risk from the precarious nature of life.

It isn't only our own anxiety that's the driving force of the urge to introduce discipline instead of allowing natural consequences to work. Our children's anxiety is also involved. In fact, their anxiety over the consequences of their actions compounds our own anxiety. I have seen how this works countless times, including with many of my clients.

Eleven-year-old Nicole used to drag her feet in the morning, frequently missing the school bus. In her mother's eagerness to protect her from facing a reprimand at school for her tardiness, she rescued Nicole by driving her to school. The more this happened, requiring the mother to alter her morning's routine, the more she began to resent Nicole's tardiness. Nevertheless, she kept up her rescuing behavior, hoping that one of her lectures en route would sink in and the next day Nicole would miraculously be on time.

The day dawned when the mother realized she was colluding with Nicole's inability to come to grips with the reality that time is limited and we need to learn how to manage it. The reason this mother was reticent to end the collusion was her own need to protect her daughter from a world in which our children constantly feel pressured. When she realized she was doing her daughter a disservice, since there are pressures in life that can't be avoided, she changed her approach. She accepted that learning to get ourselves to the school bus on time is a skill we simply have to develop; otherwise we fall into the habit of disrespecting other people's schedules.

The first thing this mother did was ask herself whether Nicole lacked the skills to organize her morning routine. Or was she sufficiently capable of managing her time but didn't see the necessity, since her mother was protecting her from the consequences? It's crucial that parents determine whether a child behaves in a particular way because of a lack of skill to handle a situation, or whether they have never felt the rub of the results of their failure to behave appropriately for the situation.

In this case, the mother discerned that Nicole did indeed have the skills to organize her morning but didn't feel the need to manage her time well because Mommy, whom she had come to regard as her chauffeur, would drive her. It became apparent the mother had set up a dynamic that was unhealthy for her daughter and only she could break it. It wasn't Nicole's fault. It was the fact the mother had interfered in her learning process by providing an artificial reality. That the mother felt resentful of having to drive her daughter should have told her this. The reality was that if Nicole missed her bus, she—not the mother—should experience the anxiety induced by her behavior.

Anxiety can't be avoided altogether, as it's a natural part of living and breathing. As infants we became anxious when we felt hungry, causing us to cry for milk. If we felt alone, rising anxiety caused us to call out for our parents to comfort us. When anxiety is experienced in a naturally induced way like this and at an optimal level, it can serve as a powerful agent of growth.

The parent's task isn't to remove anxiety but to monitor it so that it's neither too little nor overwhelming. This requires recognizing that some children are more sensitive and fragile than others, while being careful not to inject our own fears into the situation. With appropriate parental guidance, as children mature they learn to manage their anxiety. The parent needs to realize that it's not only okay for our children to experience the natural anxieties of life but actually beneficial—again, with the proviso that appropriate intervention may be needed to ensure there isn't an overload.

If a parent either unloads their own anxieties onto their children or protects them from the anxiety that accompanies the natural consequences of their behavior, they rob their children of the ability to discover their inherent resilience.

In contrast, when children feel appropriate anxiety, such as when an issue seems particularly challenging, they naturally look for solutions.

As long as this mother was willing to preempt the natural process, Nicole evaded the struggle involved in learning time management. Giving her fair warning she would no longer chauffeur her and that it was important she make the bus enabled Nicole to discover her innate organizational strengths. To prepare her for the change, the mother practiced Nicole's morning routine with her several times so they got the kinks out. This is what teaching a child involves.

It's important to realize that whenever we don't ensure our children are buffered with the appropriate skills, we set them up to fail. Instead of setting our children up, teaching sets the stage. Role playing is a valuable technique I use with both my clients' children and my own daughter to help them develop their ability to cope with different situations. You'll frequently catch me in my office repetitively enacting first days of school, social situations, homework management, and bedtime rituals. Through practice, children become adept at handling their circumstances.

When Nicole awakened on the morning she was expected to be on time for her bus, her mother engaged in none of her usual interfering behavior of helping her daughter finish things on time. Leaving everything to Nicole, she stepped aside. Not surprisingly the girl missed the bus. Instead of rushing in, coat on and car keys in hand, the mother lounged in her pajamas sipping her cup of coffee. It took a minute for Nicole to realize that Mommy wasn't going to drive her this morning. Panic set in and the waterworks went into action as she sobbed, "Mommy, what will happen to me? I'll be in trouble. You need to help me." Although it was uncomfortable to watch her anxiety rise, the mother knew it was important for Nicole to register the natural consequence of her tardiness. She let her daughter sit with her discomfort for a good five minutes, connecting cause and effect for her—not in a judgmental way, but in a soothing tone. She then suggested, "Let's brainstorm some solutions."

After a few moments Nicole said matter-of-factly, "School has already started, so I guess I will just have to go into the office and get a late pass." Nicole got a late pass that day and has never missed the bus again.

The reason Nicole learned in one day what her mother had been unable to teach her over a period of weeks is that the mother took herself out of the equation, which allowed the natural consequence to emerge—and there's no better teacher. I find that many parents are unwilling to do this because they are heavily invested in their image as "the good parent" who would never let their children suffer. If only they saw the irony of their position! As long as they would rather buffer their child against the anxiety of facing the consequences of their actions, they deny the child the chance to let life spur them to grow. Couple this with all the yelling and reprimanding that takes place, and both the child's and the parent's anxiety go through the roof.

I tell those parents who constantly drive their children to school because they are late, that if they aren't willing to allow the consequences to take effect, they should at least drive their child to school calmly and without complaining. To berate our children for their behavior while aiding and abetting it is to compound the damage we are doing.

What we are talking about is *consistency*. Books about discipline emphasize consistency. I, too, want to emphasize consistency. But I mean something very different from what most of these books are talking about. Parents take consistency to mean they need to persistently assert their will. But consistency isn't a matter of how often we tell our children what to do. Rather, consistency means that what we are saying is consistent with our deepest feelings and the reality of the situation.

Consistency requires clarity about our intentions and alignment with the reality of the situation. When we are aligned with the "as is," our words carry a natural authority.

With Nicole and the school bus, the mother was neither clear about her intentions nor aligned with reality. This is why she was wishy-washy, oscillating between being upset with Nicole and wanting to protect her. The mother's anxiety kept her from seeing the natural consequences of her daughter's behavior, though they were staring her in the face. She had been giving her daughter double messages, which is devastating to our children. How can we teach them if we continually contradict ourselves? Only to the degree that our interactions with our children are conscious, instead of being driven by our own confusion, can we teach effectively.

> To berate our children for their behavior while aiding and abetting it is to compound the damage we are doing.

Once parents realize that artificial impositions are fundamentally different from natural consequences, it's important for them to identify the natural consequences in any given situation, then exercise consistency in allowing the consequences to have their effect. For example, if a child paints on the wall, effective correction doesn't mean we take away the child's paints or computer time. Instead we go with what the situation naturally calls for, which is that the child learns how to clean the wall and paint on the appropriate surface. If a child doesn't eat, they go hungry unless both they and the parent create new solutions for meal choices that work for both. If a child doesn't do homework, they have to deal with their teacher the next day and possibly miss recess. If a child doesn't fall asleep, they will have to wake up on time the next day and deal with their own grogginess.

As you can see, in each instance the consequence emerges naturally from the situation and teaches the child through direct feedback from their environment. There's no better teacher than direct and immediate feedback. Artificial "discipline" can never match its effectiveness. Really, the solutions are simple. It's the execution that's difficult—but only because we have been conditioned to parent by disciplining instead of allowing consequences to do their work.

A situation with my client Judy exemplifies this. She came to me complaining of problems with her teenage son, who had begun to engage in risky behavior. "Why does he do such stupid things?" she demanded. I explained that what was happening now was the result of years of rescuing him from the natural consequences of his actions. His present dangerous behavior was simply the culmination of lots of missed opportunities to allow him to learn cause and effect as situations arose.

It so happened a perfect opportunity to begin to pair cause and effect presented itself at this juncture. Judy had spent hours preparing a fun weekend at the beach for her son and his friend, which she was really looking forward to. But even though her son was aware it was illegal for him to drive, the night before the event he snuck out of the house, borrowed his mother's car without permission, and ended up in a minor accident.

Judy now felt torn. The car still ran, but it wasn't in good enough shape to go to the beach. Should she drop it off at the shop and rent a car for the weekend? On the one hand she was invested in her image of herself as the fun parent who had planned a great time for her son, while on the other it was obvious her son needed to experience the natural—not punitive—consequences of his actions.

When Judy called me for help, it was obvious she was overlooking the vital organic teaching tool of allowing cause and effect to play out in their most natural way. Indeed, her long-established habit of intervening to avert the effect had contributed to the present crisis. With this in mind, I directed her attention to the essential question: "Whose need are you serving right now by going to the beach? Yours, or your son's?"

I explained, "While you are well intentioned as a parent wanting to take him for a great time at the beach, things have now changed. He has exhibited behavior that requires a different response from you. Not a punitive one, but one that teaches him through the natural consequences of his behavior. If you rented a car to go to the beach, he wouldn't experience the repercussions of taking the family car without permission."

Judy was able to see that, regardless of her desires, her son needed to experience the consequences of his actions. This is what was required for his emotional development, no matter how hard it was for her to execute. It can be terribly disappointing for a parent to allow consequences to have their effect, but it's essential to be consistent. Even though it was hard for Judy to let go of her agenda, she knew she must cancel the trip and take the car to be repaired that day. Otherwise her son would learn he could behave irresponsibly without consequences.

When a child's behavior isn't up to par, parents feel they need to "do" something—whether rescuing them, punishing them, bribing them, or in some other way intervening. In contrast, exposing our children to natural consequences requires us to step back from so much doing, while actively monitoring how life is teaching our children and providing encouragement and guidance when they require it.

Chapter 6

Rudeness, Biting, and Hitting: How to Make Your Child's Limits Clear

When my daughter Maia's friend Sarah told her she couldn't come to Maia's birthday party because she had been rude to her parents, Maia exclaimed in the most apropos way, "What's that got to do with my party?"

Later Maia asked me, "Mommy, would you ever do that to me?"

I replied, "Why would I? That makes no sense."

"I feel so bad for Sarah," Maia added. "Her mom is just being mean."

Maia's insight needs to reach deep into our hearts. Children can spot the injustice of our arbitrary ways of interacting with them. The truth is, many parents are indeed mean to their children. But they don't recognize their meanness because they camouflage it as "teaching my child to behave."

Maia and I talked about how I would have responded

had Maia shown the same rudeness to me. "We would talk about it, addressing your rudeness right there and then," I explained.

Said Maia, "You mean like the other day when I slammed my bedroom door because I was mad at you, and we talked about it, and I wrote about it in my journal?"

"Exactly," I said.

Rudeness isn't a matter of "badness." To treat the child as if they are bad when they are rude is to miss the real issue. Instead, the child needs to learn that rudeness isn't an effective way of relating and won't get them what they want. Instead of attacking back when a child is rude, or punishing them, we need to disengage from their rudeness. The child then learns there's no payoff in such behavior. They don't achieve what they are trying to achieve.

When we don't make behavior such as being sassy or bratty a moral issue but keep it entirely on a practical plain, we teach children to be practical. They learn that relationships thrive when there's mutual respect. They realize it's important to ask politely for the things they want instead of demanding, since politeness is one of the ways we respect people.

In all human relationships, limits are necessary. Limits define what works and what doesn't in terms of the effect we have on each other. Learning appropriate limits is therefore a vital part of a child's development. Often referred to as "boundaries," limits need to be practical, clear, and consistent. Once the limits in any relationship or situation are established, all parties need to stick to them.

Of course, when someone violates us in a deeply hurtful manner, our instinct is to limit the other's freedom in some manner. This is a natural push back. What we are doing when we push back is attempting a boundary, since there appears to be none. Much errant adult behavior comes down to boundary violations. For this reason, setting appropriate limits is essential to effective parenting. When we teach boundaries empathically and consistently, the need for discipline evaporates.

To illustrate how this works, consider the issue of cleanliness. Part of respect for other people, not to mention for ourselves, is that we keep ourselves clean so we neither look nor smell offensive to others. This means that even if a child cries and cries that they don't want to bathe, the parent needs to function as a safe container in which the child's antagonism to bathing can be expressed, while holding to the need for cleanliness as nonnegotiable. The child doesn't get to do anything or go anywhere until they have bathed, and no battles need to be fought to make the point.

The need for cleanliness is fundamentally no different from the need for politeness. When a child violates our boundaries by being rude, the child needs to experience the consequence of such a boundary violation. What is the natural consequence? Depending on the situation, it might be for the parent to walk away, thereby removing themselves from the violation. When the parent disengages themselves in such a manner, they define a clear limit: this behavior will not be tolerated.

Limits set in a consistent yet empathic manner have greater teaching value than any punishment ever could. Of course, for the parent to be both consistent *and* loving during such limit setting is the key. It takes stamina to create and hold to such limits when a child protests or has angry outbursts.

This is when it's essential that parents function as containers for such emotional reactivity.

If a child's behavior toward us is inappropriate, it's the child's way of expressing the need for one of two things: connect with me, or contain me. Unfortunately, what tends to happen is the opposite: when our boundaries are crossed, we then invade our child's boundaries. They hit us, so we hit them. They are rude to us, so we yell at them and shame them. Such tit-for-tat reactivity destroys connection.

Whenever a child is being rude, we need to determine whether they are in a calm enough state to talk directly about the rudeness or whether we need to allow them time to cool off. If the child needs to calm down, the parent can simply walk away—calmly and non-reactively. The child then experiences the natural consequence of losing the companionship of the parent until they are able to talk in a polite way. Once the child is ready to restore the lost companionship, we then talk about how rudeness isn't a constructive way to communicate.

When our children are rude, disrespectful, hit us, or bite, the issue is always one of inadequate limits. Either the child is starving for connection and angry about it, or the parent has failed to establish adequate boundaries and the child feels free to violate the parent's personhood.

Connection and respect for each other's boundaries are both essential to healthy development. They go hand in hand, each building on the other. Children have to learn how to be closely connected, respecting the boundaries of others—and, equally important, how to respond appropriately when their own boundaries are violated.

When I say children have to "learn," let me be clear what

I mean. The word "learn" is one we tend to pronounce with great emphasis, since we believe this means we need to lecture. The reality is that children learn not because we *tell* them, but from how we *relate* to them. It's the difference between "doing to" versus "doing with."

The first task of any parent is to establish connection. If the parent has established a strong connection with their child, they will be able to expose their child to the natural consequences of their behavior with ease and confidence. Without such a strong connection, the parent is likely to feel riddled with anxiety and guilt—the two emotions that mess up natural learning. A child who is rude, or who bites or hits, because they are starved for connection can't learn about appropriate boundaries until the connection is cemented.

If an older child is being inordinately rude the parent might say, "It's clear we are unable to discuss this right now, so I'm going to leave you alone for a moment. When we are relaxed enough to talk civilly together, we can continue our conversation." This involves no shaming or blaming, only cause and effect. But again, if this is said punitively, it will lose its power and even backfire. There must be no emotional "charge" to what the parent says or the child will pick up on this. Then the child will resent the parent and be glad to be away from them, rather than wanting to restore communication.

When walking away is called for, it often terrifies parents because they think they are abandoning their child. But if it's done calmly, not reactively, to walk away becomes a powerful attractant. By "attractant," I mean that our calmness conveys a great sense of presence on our part—and presence is a powerful draw. It grabs the person's attention more than anything we can say. Instead of feeling abandoned when we walk away, the child feels the loss of our presence and wants to restore it.

To accomplish this, the parent needs real presence of mind. There can't be any emotional distancing in the parent's actions, even at a subtle level. Walking away mustn't have any emotional overtones but must be purely practical. Only in this way does it function as a natural consequence. When the parent walks away but retains complete openness to the child, the parent's presence is missed.

The most powerful tool any of us has at our disposal is our personal presence. Children sit up and pay attention when they experience the power of our presence. Yet so much of the time we relate to them not from presence but from old habits. We aren't truly "here" for our children. We are just saying or doing something to get them off our back. It's this internal conflict between what we do on a surface level and what we feel on a subconscious level that creates the problems we encounter with our children. If it weren't for this, we would simply be so present with them that they would know we mean business.

The important thing to realize is that boundaries aren't established by mere words but are formed at an energetic level. How we carry ourselves, how we treat ourselves, who we surround ourselves with, and what we allow speak far more loudly than our insistence that our children "respect" us. In other words, boundaries such as politeness, not biting, and not hitting are being negotiated from the moment a child comes into our life.

Chapter 7

Your Children Are Here to Challenge Your Integrity

Many parents say to me, "I love my child so much. I do so much for them. Yet they are always angry with me." Or a parent may say, "No matter how much I sacrifice for my child, they are so disrespectful."

The reason for this is that, though the parent is acting a particular way on the surface, a quite different script is being played out at the subconscious level. It's the vibes from this hidden script that the child is picking up on, leading them to believe they can act this way. Our children see how we relate to ourselves and our life, and this is what they absorb.

When our children are disrespectful to us, at a subconscious level we have given them permission to be so. This means some part of us is comfortable with the disrespect. Somewhere in our childhood we internalized the idea it's okay for people to disrespect us. Our children pick up on this.

I think of a mother who discovered the reason her children weren't listening to her despite her yelling, threats, and bribes was that at a subconscious level she didn't see herself as a leader. Growing up as the youngest of four, she was always more the follower and pleaser than the leader. As a result, despite her threats, her children picked up that she didn't mean a word she said and was uncomfortable with being in charge. When her children didn't listen to her, it confirmed her childhood understanding of her role. It was essential she quit replaying this role.

We can begin to see how our children's "problematic behavior" originates from a different place than is commonly thought. From my clinical experience, I would have to say the majority of child dysfunction originates from lack of awareness of the dynamics our children are triggering in us from our own past.

Our subconscious patterns hold tremendous energy. This energy causes us to create an atmosphere our children react to. We could say they pick up our emotional "vibes." I liken these vibes to the air we breathe, in that they are pervasive yet invisible. Because they work in an energetic manner, often running counter to our words and actions, they can be difficult to recognize.

We don't realize the power of these vibes, but they set the stage for every experience, interaction, and relationship in which we participate. In other words, contrary to what we would like to believe, our children don't respond to our surface instructions. Instead they are attuned to our sub-conscious script—the very script we ourselves may not be aware of.

We might liken these subconscious vibes to a magnet, attracting or repelling without any conscious awareness on our part of what's happening. Because our children are dependent on us, they are extremely sensitive to the vibes we emit. This sets up a dynamic between ourselves and our children. The entry point to this dynamic is always the parent's subconscious, with its magnetic energy.

The key to effective parenting is to turn the spotlight away from the child as "behaving badly" to our own "badly behaving emotionality." Unless we identify and untangle our emotional patterns, we will unwittingly foster dysfunctional behavior in our children. We will search high and low for ways to fix our children, not realizing there's nothing to fix, only a need for us to grow ourselves up.

We can see how this works in practice in the case of a parent who said to me, "My kid is forever pouting. You can't tell me it's *me* who causes that. How can I be responsible? Isn't this just my kid's temperament?"

"You are right in that you aren't responsible for your child's inherent temperament," I agreed. "Every child comes into the world with their own unique makeup. In that sense you aren't responsible. Your responsibility lies elsewhere." Understanding the "elsewhere" is crucial.

From the moment of a child's arrival in our lives, their makeup interacts with ours, either flowing or clashing, until it becomes impossible to detect what's purely temperament and what's emerging from the child's interaction with us and their environment. We can't say something is purely "the way my child is," such as "my child is a type A personality" or "my child is naturally cranky," since both

> **Unless we identify and untangle our emotional patterns, we will unwittingly foster dysfunctional behavior in our children.**

parent and child are constantly shaping each other in the dynamic of parenting.

As a parent, where we come into the picture is in our *response*. In the case of a child who pouts a lot, we either mitigate the pouting or amplify it. Whether we mitigate or amplify their pouting depends on how it affects us. Children pick up on this instantly and it's this that most influences them.

It's challenging to take responsibility for the vibes we put out and the ways they affect our children. For one thing, these vibes are hard to observe since they occur at a nonverbal, subtle energetic level. A willingness to turn the spotlight inward, instead of focusing on our children's actions, helps us shift from being a faultfinder to becoming an ally and guide.

A particularly poignant illustration of this is school grades. We may tell our children, "Grades aren't that important; all that matters is that you try your best." However, most of us have been culturally indoctrinated to worry about grades, since we consider them a barometer of our child's success. No matter what we say, our child picks up on how we react every time they come home with less than an A. The child is watching our body language, our facial expressions, the way our brow furrows, the narrowing of our eyes. Despite our attempts to cover up our reactions, our anxiety always seeps through.

When we have resolved an issue in our own life, we are no longer anxious about it but are at peace with it. Anxiety springs from those issues that have gone unresolved. Perhaps grades were a big deal when we were growing up. Though on an intellectual level we know they are a poor predictor of a child's future success and that many of the world's highest achievers never excelled in school, on an emotional level most of us still have issues around grades. Our children pick up on this just as we picked up on it with our parents. It may manifest as performance anxiety during tests, stomachaches, headaches, or any manner of afflictions. Regardless of the precise manifestation, which will be largely governed by the child's particular temperament, the anxiety will surface. Thus it is that families repeat emotional themes from generation to generation.

I think of Alexandra, a parent who presented me with her greatest challenge—daily battles over when electronics should be turned off. "This has been going on nonstop for a year," she bemoaned. The moment we find ourselves in a pattern that lasts more than a few days, we can be sure its roots go deep into our own childhood. The reason patterns stick around is because they bring up emotions within us that are familiar. Uncomfortable though these emotions may be, they act as a comfort zone in that they are what we are used to.

When I pointed out to Alexandra she was inviting conflict, she asked, "How can I want conflict? It's impossible I would want this. I hate it. I just don't know how to end it." But as we dug deeper, she came to realize her conflict with her children rose out of her own inner conflict. She hated when her children took advantage of her good nature, yet the vibes she put out were ones of needing to please—a replica of how she felt around her domineering, hard-to-please mother. Desperate for her mother's attention, she was always bending over backwards to get it.

When parents come to me with problems with their

children, my first area of exploration is always the parents. Like Alexandra, parents are shocked when I begin with them. However, I'm eventually able to show them how their unresolved feelings from childhood are still in operation—so much so that they are the leading contributor to how their own children function in similar situations in their lives.

> All conflict with our children originates with our own internal subconscious conflicts.

Eventually my clients come to the realization that *all conflict with our children originates with our own internal subconscious conflicts.* This may at first be hard for some of us to swallow. But as one astute reviewer of this book prior to publication commented, "There was a time I would have disagreed with 'all.' That time has passed."

Let's take the example of junk food. If a parent finds themselves in constant battles because their child wants to eat at McDonald's all the time, it's important to recognize that, at some level, their craving for this kind of food came from the parent's endorsement of it. The choice of McDonald's as a meal option was sanctioned by the parent when the child noticed the parent ate junk food.

Perhaps a parent doesn't eat junk food regularly. They may even subscribe to the notion that to eat at McDonald's is unhealthy, a point they no doubt make to their child. However, their words barely register because what their child picks up on is the fact that when they are in a hurry, stressed, or in need of comfort food, they readily drive to the Golden Arches. Once their child internalizes the clash between their words and their actions, naturally she or he milks it to their advantage.

"Don't do it," a parent says. However, the real message is, "If you do, nothing of any real consequence will happen. After all, I sometimes do it too." The parent is conveying the sense that, for all their protesting, they are subconsciously okay with this behavior. Even a lack of willpower in such matters is rooted in the subconscious. This is how our subconscious undermines our best intentions. Unless we realize that most conflict with our children is sourced in this kind of internal clash with ourselves, we make the surface issue our focus. This leads to interminable battles. Discipline, which wasn't even in the picture, now takes center stage as we seek to control the monster we ourselves created.

Once we understand the subtle manner in which our unconscious baggage plays out, we realize that much of our children's misbehavior is a pushback against a situation we've set up. Punishment is therefore totally inappropriate, since the problem didn't start with our children. In the case of a child who wants to eat junk all the time, the habit started with the double message we gave them when we said that junk food is bad yet ate it anyway. A child's demand for McDonald's reflects the fact we didn't take the time to develop an awareness of the need to eat healthily—and which we didn't follow ourselves.

If a child wants to eat McDonald's every day or play on X-Box for hours on end, the parent needs to recognize that these may be substitutes for their not being present in the moment—a habit children learn from us. They can be forms of distraction from what children are actually experiencing, actually feeling. In the case of eating junk as a way of avoiding feeling, we say in the vernacular that we are "stuffing our feelings down." The subtle art of distraction is learned when the child sees their parent practicing distraction instead of dealing with whatever it is they are seeking to avoid.

Take the parent who, feeling anxious, lights a cigarette. The cigarette distracts them from their anxiety. The person believes they are "doing something" about their anxiety, when all they are really doing is temporarily allaying it. Or consider the parent who turns to food or alcohol as a way to reduce their stress, subconsciously sending out the vibe that they are unable to manage their emotions without a substance. The child learns to handle stress in the same way.

Then there's the mother who spends thirty minutes a day donning makeup and kvetching before the mirror about how bad she looks, thus unwittingly sending the message that looks are a barometer of self-worth. Meanwhile, the father begrudges his work and complains nonstop about his boss, long hours, and heavy workload, unknowingly sending the message that work is drudgery and something to be resisted. The father's complaining distracts his attention from facing up to a situation he resists coming to terms with. Our children pick up on all these vibes and incorporate them into their own repertoire.

When a parent's actions match their intent, they are able to engage their children in an honest way. Children brought up with this kind of communication know they can rely on their parents to follow the same principles they are asking of their children, which creates a culture in the home to which everyone subscribes. For example, children are far more likely to do such basic things as making their bed each morning when they see their parents make theirs.

Our children absorb our ways constantly. They are always watching, listening, making a mental note of what we are doing and how we do it. As a new mother, to realize all my choices now had bearing on another human being felt like a heavy burden to bear. Whether I ordered a diet soda or water, fries or salad, worked out or vegged out in front of the television, nothing was simply about me anymore. How I used my time, coped with anxiety, handled failure, related to my spouse, took care of my finances—everything now affected how another human being would eventually lead her own life.

Could I handle this much responsibility? I discovered that what initially felt hard to bear paid off in a peaceful household in which joy and love prevailed, not constant battles over "discipline."

Chapter 8

How to Say "Yes" or "No" Effectively

A mother complained to me, "I hate the way my children use such bad language. They use the S word, the B word, even the F word, and I can't stand it. We never use this language in our house. I don't know where they picked it up."

"When you communicate your displeasure over the language they use, how do you do it?" I asked.

"I tell them not to use such words," she said.

"And how often have you done this?"

"Oh, over and over, till I'm sick of telling them."

"So let me ask you: If your children were hitting you, would you simply tell them over and over not to hit you, while they keep on doing it despite your objection?"

"Of course not. I'd make it clear hitting me is unacceptable."

"And would your children listen?"

"When I talk in that tone? Yes. They know I mean business."

"In other words, much of the time you don't really mean what you say—and your children know it."

Parents bemoan, "The minute I say 'no' to my child, she pitches a fit. But if I say 'yes,' there's no problem. How can I say 'no' and have my child accept my decision?" It surprises them when I tell them it's not a matter of yes versus no. The issue is whether the child feels the parent is truly aligned with their decision. When parents are clear about the purpose of their yes or no and can communicate this, the child responds appropriately.

How often do we say "yes" to our children without really thinking through what we are saying? Our "yes" isn't a meaningful yes that's said with all the factors of the present situation in mind, but is more of an off-the-cuff thoughtless reaction that's a reflection of our mood rather than what the situation calls for. Because our "yes" isn't an authentic yes, children quickly realize it's arbitrary. Similarly, because we say "no" a lot of the time when there's really no reason to say no, this too feels random to the child. Consequently, yes and no have no real meaning, which means they can be argued with and changed for the sake of peace if the child pushes hard enough.

When parents don't buy into their family policies, they fail to inspire their children to do so. Little wonder children keep pushing their parent's buttons to test whether they mean what they say. For instance, a child asks for an iPod Touch because all their friends have one. The parent feels the child doesn't need one, believing the novelty will wear off. However, wanting to please the child, and not clear about their own convictions, the parent yields to the demands.

The parent would do better to say, "I really hear that you want an iPod. Let's discuss why this is important to you. If we can both agree this will enhance your life in a positive manner, we'll find a way for you to obtain one. This may mean you pay for part of it and I pay for part of it. We also need to agree on guidelines for how you'll use it."

When such a dialogue occurs, the child begins to understand that things aren't given or denied randomly, but that there's always a serious thought process behind the decision to give or deny. Through the consistent use of such meaningful conversations, children come to feel their parents are allied with them.

When there's a mutually agreed-upon expectation around something of this nature, the parent isn't thrust into the role of policing it. The parent ensures that the child is sufficiently mature to maintain their side of the agreement. If the child isn't mature enough and the parent still decides to enter into this agreement, they need to be fully aware of the muck that will be stirred up when their expectations aren't followed. Thus it's imperative parents do their own emotional homework before saying "yes" or "no" to their children.

When a parent's own life manifests integrity, children are far better able to accept "no" when it's required. The child understands the parent isn't saying no merely to flex their muscles. Because any arbitrariness in terms of our "yes" or "no" has been eliminated from the equation, children learn to trust there's always a solid reason for the parent's decisions, which invites them to buy into these decisions.

To give a child things or deprive them because to do so matches our subconscious agenda—our unresolved emotional baggage—rather than aligning with their developmental needs, is to court conflict. But if we are clear about the purpose of our decisions, aware of both our own and our child's agenda, though the child may not like what

To give a child things or deprive them because to do so matches our subconscious agenda—our unresolved emotional baggage—rather than aligning with their developmental needs, is to court conflict.

they hear, they will be able to respect the fact we are acting with integrity.

A parent complains, "My son begged me for an X-Box and now I can't get him off it, which leads to endless battles." Another parent says, "My daughter pleaded with me to let her have a TV in her room. Now I yell at her day and night to turn it off." Such acts of seeming kindness toward our children quickly turn into a source of conflict.

In these situations I respond, "Do you know why you gave these electronics to your child? Was there a clearly defined reason for them?"

They sheepishly respond, "Everyone has them. My kid feels left out if they don't have them."

"Just because everyone has them isn't a reason for you to buy them for your child," I explain. "If you feel your child is going to be overstimulated or become addicted to the technology, you aren't helping the situation. The reason to buy anything is if it enhances your child's wellbeing and your life as a family."

I learned long ago not to bow to pressure—either my daughter's or that of society. What "other" families may be doing has nothing to do with my decisions as one responsible for bringing up my daughter. In our culture where peer pressure, the school, the mall, television, and the internet exert so much influence, it's crucial we make decisions that affect our children based on our own internal compass. Our decisions need to come from the heart, not from pressure. In this way our "yes" is truly a green light, while our "no" absolutely means "stop"—and our children fall in line because they feel the powerful presence of a heart that's aligned with reality.

Of course, being human, I may even become exasperated if my daughter nags constantly—though this won't change my decision since it's been well thought out. In due course she'll learn I'm not being mean, but that there's a valid reason for my "no." I could easily say "yes" to Maia for the sake of "peace" and to please her, but what feels easy and makes us comfortable has nothing to do with good parenting. It's a matter of being clear about what our children need for their emotional development.

Hence when people say to me, "My child is on the internet all the time," I explain that the internet isn't the problem. The electronics themselves are never the problem. It's the lack of clarity over the purpose of the electronics that's the issue. Arbitrarily telling our children they can or can't watch a show, can or can't go on the internet, undercuts our "yes" or "no," rendering these meaningless.

Clarity begins with the parent. Ask yourself, where do you stand with electronics? Is your own relationship with these gadgets ambivalent? For instance, on the one hand you might abhor their influence in your children's lives, yet on the other you perhaps find yourself on Facebook every chance you get.

You may tell your child to "get off the computer," yet that may be precisely what you turn on for them as a babysitter whenever you don't want them to interrupt you—in effect communicating that whether they can or can't use a particular form of electronics depends on your mood. Is it any wonder that a child pitches a fit when we say "no" for an entirely arbitrary reason? It isn't the "no" in itself that's the problem, but how we utilize it.

The key is for the parent to buy into the "yes" or the "no" at the deeper level of their intent. The "yes" or the "no" must be purposeful. Purposeful not just to impose control, but because it's truly what the situation requires. The "yes" or the "no" are then aligned with the "as is" of the situation.

For example, we all believe we shouldn't eat with our feet. Is this up for negotiation? Do our children need to be coerced or rewarded to get them to follow convention in the way they eat? No, they pick it up from the consistency of our modeling.

Speaking of buying into things, money is one of those elements where parents often feel guilty and operate out of a false sense of self instead of what's best for the family.

In a case where a family is strapped for cash, it's crucial this is integrated into the whole family's awareness so that no one pretends otherwise. This is one of those realities of life that, unless the family comes into wealth in some way, is nonnegotiable. Since in most cases a family's financial situation tends to improve only gradually, it's prudent to get everyone on board with how things are. The wise use of money then becomes a family value, which children pick up on at an early age. Children may not like the fact they can't have some of the luxuries other children in their circle enjoy. However, they don't have to like it. There are many things in life we may not like, but they are nevertheless realities.

Manipulation comes into play when we try to coerce our children into believing they *should* like something when they don't, or should dislike something when they in fact like it, while not allowing them the freedom to express their feelings. In the case of money, if we are clear about our financial situation and detached from a need to appear more affluent than we are, we won't be shaken by our children's discontent. We can allow them to express this discontent without either shaming them or bending to their will.

If we have subconscious issues around money, these issues will play out in our dealings with our children. If we are conflicted, our children will be conflicted. They will constantly want things we can't afford because, lacking clarity within ourselves, we give them the impression we can afford things when we really can't. Our children may also see us spend money on ourselves—or on them—that we said we "don't have."

The heart of the matter is clarity. The first step to clarity is to take stock of our reality. Have *we* accepted our reality? Until we can, our children won't accept it either, which will result in whining and complaining. They have learned that if they whine enough, we may give in. Picking up on our inner conflict, they are experts at exploiting it. The simple fact is that our internal doublespeak about money is far more powerful than what we say, since it's our vibes that most influence our children—vibes that, in this case, convey the message there might be money for what they want if they are persistent. When they don't receive what they want, not really understanding the reason, they resent us. In this way we fuel negative behavior.

Unless we come to terms with our reality, we can't be

transparent with our children in this way—and this is when we resort to manipulation. Parents then deliver messages such as, "You are being so greedy, you should be ashamed of yourself. Don't you know that money doesn't grow on trees? You seem to think we are made of money." Shaming our children for their honest desires in this way, we dishonor their feelings. A practical matter has become a personal issue, with the parent feeling frustrated and the child rejected.

Our children have every right to want things—this is normal and healthy. It indicates they have a connection to their lives. It doesn't necessarily imply they are greedy. It is however unhealthy when a child believes their self-worth is tied to these objects of their desire. It's essential for parents to understand what purpose something will serve in their child's life so they don't simply give into demands without a clear sense of limits.

The key is to know our reality so well, and what our assets and limitations are, that a conflict between the family's needs and the child's desires doesn't escalate into a battle. "I fully understand where you are coming from," we might tell our image-conscious teen, "but we as a family don't believe it's necessary to spend $300 on a pair of sneakers. I know how much you want them. However, if they are so important to you, we will help you create a plan so you can buy them yourself." In this way we honor our child's feelings while also acquainting them with the family's reality.

In a situation of this kind, the most important thing we teach a child is that not only do they have a right to their desires, but that as part of their universe we will fully assist them in meeting these desires if they are willing to work for them. In this way we teach them to have goals. They also learn that no matter how difficult a goal might be to accomplish, every goal has the potential to be achieved through partnership, communication, and work. Our children learn that they are active co-creators in their universe, able to actualize their dreams through action. Such children grow up to make good decisions in life. When we honor our children at this level, engaging in a meaningful manner with their desires, they move away from being passive recipients of our dictates and into an active role in their own lives. Such potential moments of conflict then become opportunities to learn how to be an active co-creator of their own reality and destiny.

Each moment with our child is a reflection of the past and a foundation for the future.

This level of engagement doesn't emerge overnight. It involves an energy that a parent brings into every interaction with their child, especially those harrowing moments when the parent's need to control is threatened. Each moment with our child is a reflection of the past and a foundation for the future. Every "yes" or "no" needs to be part of a coherent flow, not said out of the blue for no real reason. A child raised with such consistency is no longer driven to either comply or defy. They live in harmony with the "as is" of reality.

Chapter 9

You're Not a Moviemaker

We each run a movie in our head of the way life is supposed to be. We cast our children and intimate others in roles we want for them, with little regard for whether they have consented to these roles. We impose our script on them, never really stopping to examine whether they are fitted for the part.

With strangers, and perhaps to a lesser degree our friends, we restrain ourselves when it comes to directing the movie. We know that if we impose on them too much, they'll simply walk out of our life. But in the case of our children, who are hostage to our care, we feel free to write the lines, buy the costumes, and predict the conclusion of the movie.

If suffocated in their assigned roles, our children have only two options. They can comply, taking on the role in which they have been cast, and in the process abandon their true self. Or they can fight back at the risk of being crushed anyway. In how a child responds to these two options lie all the behavioral issues we face as parents.

So attached are we to our subconscious movies, spending a lifetime budget on them, that we fight tooth and nail to manifest them. When these movies don't do well at the box office—or, even more disappointing, don't even make it to production—we are devastated. Many of us rant, rave, scream, and blame everyone in sight. Of course, the most ready targets are our children.

I've often observed the way my subconscious movies play out in my own home. In one of these movies I cast myself as the Iron Chef, winning a global contest in gourmet cooking. One afternoon I was inspired to make a vegetable lasagna for my daughter. I then decided she would enjoy it for an afternoon snack. After all, how many mothers prepare a multi-layered home-cooked lasagna for a meager afternoon snack?

When Maia arrived, I was excited to showcase my work. "Ta dah!" I announced, unveiling my creation.

Maia took one look at it and said, "What's *that?* I'm not eating *that.*"

"Wrong lines!" I wanted to yell. "Repeat after me: 'Wow, Mom, that looks amazing! I'm so blessed that my mother is one of the best cooks in the world.'"

While my gut was chanting, "I slaved at this lasagna to make it really tasty for her, and all I get is ingratitude," Maia skipped away to do her own thing, leaving me staring at my creation.

In that moment an awareness came to me—almost an out-of-body experience. I saw my lonely, pitiful self on stage under the spotlight in front of an empty theater. I saw how I had constructed this entire scene in my head and even called it "Sacrifice and Glory." I saw my subconscious obsession with wanting to please, which of course came from my longing to feel validated both as a person and in the role of mother. At that moment I knew I had a choice. I could pretend that none of this was a movie of my making and blame Maia for slighting me, or I could enter into my deeper, feeling self—the real me, separate from my role in my movie, which would allow me to connect to Maia as a real human being, not as a daughter who "ought to be appreciative of everything I do for her."

Had I allowed my subconscious to rule me, my usual approach would have been to sermonize. I would have severely reprimanded her: "You are such a rude child! How can you be so disrespectful? Don't you know people are starving in Africa? Don't you realize how hard I worked on this special treat for you?"

What lay behind my impulse to finger-point, blame, and put her down, shriveling her to feel the smallness I was feeling? Simply my need to feel powerful again, reinstating the hierarchical relationship, solidified in my role as mother. Who cares that Maia would be crushed to bits? Who cares that the lesson she would receive from the incident would be that she can't be real, and that to be authentic is unsafe and will get you punished?

The Iron Chef is one of my many movies. For instance, I have the Martyred Mommy movie, in various renditions:

I'm Always Busy

I'm Exhausted

I Do Everything in this House

Why Is it Only My Child Who's So Difficult?

This Always Happens to Me

I'm So Zen and Conscious Until My Family Walks in the Door.

My friends have also shared their personal favorite movies with me:

Children Must Listen at All Costs

Education Is the Most Important Thing

My Childhood Sucked but My Kids Have It Lucky

I Slave 24/7 So My Children Will Have a Better Life than I Did.

These themes become our background chant. Because they have been playing for so many years, they are almost like our skin, so much a part of us that we hardly notice them. Because they are an intricate part of our psyche, we rarely stop to question their validity. Were we to examine them, we would notice that we always cast ourselves as the most virtuous, patient, giving, and sacrificing. The other party is always the one at fault.

In the case of my performance as Iron Chef and my lasagna creation, I happen to have a strong-willed daughter who speaks up for herself. Partly that's her nature and partly it's a pattern of behavior that reflects how her father and I engage with the world, which has reinforced her own tendency. Had I disciplined her, she would have reacted forcefully, perhaps announcing, "I *told* you I don't want to eat this. Stop forcing me!" We would have entered into the back-and-forth of combat.

"Don't you dare use that tone of voice with me," I would have fumed.

"Mommy, stop saying these things," she would scream. "I'm not doing anything wrong—you are."

At this point I would have resorted to the universal discipline technique of "timeout." Utilizing this approach, my reaction would have been, "Go to your room, young lady, until you learn some manners!"

This is considered to be a tried-and-tested technique by most authors I have ever read on the child discipline question. However, the belief that this approach works is an illusion. On one level it may seem to calm the situation, but what's really happening is that the problem is being deferred. Avoiding the issue doesn't solve it. On the contrary, it perpetuates a problem that didn't even need to exist in the first place.

How can I claim there wasn't a problem to begin with? It all started with the creation of my movie, my idea of how things should be. Maia's response wasn't the problem. Rather the problem was that I didn't *like* how she responded. Because she didn't follow my script and stroke my ego, I could have made it an issue. For her daring to stray from her mother's expectations, in my mind she deserved some form of discipline.

I was about to enter into a drama that would have involved complete disregard for Maia's authentic self. Had I entered the drama, what was important to my daughter would hardly have featured in my thinking, so wrapped up would I have become in my idea of myself as the gourmet chef. When Maia dared to bare her soul, stating her feelings, I was tempted to ride roughshod over her right to claim her truth. To have done so would have robbed her of her realness.

As I mentioned, my daughter is strong-willed. What if I had a child who was naturally more submissive? This child would most likely have cowered at my reprimand and complied with my demand. Burying her own desires, she would have eaten my lasagna and even paid homage to my narcissistic hunger to be praised. I would have achieved my goal of getting my way, but at what cost? It would have come at the price of her authenticity. She would have learned that people can override her feelings—not only her mother, but later in life others who might even seriously maltreat her. Is it any wonder so many girls grow up to be victims of abusive men?

You may be thinking, "But a child has to learn to eat whatever is put in front of them. A child can't demand croissants when there's only toast in the house." It's true that a child can't have what isn't available. However, when we set aside our controlling ego, we can certainly make the toast the way our children enjoy it. In this way parenting becomes a cooperative venture in which the needs of both parent and child are taken into account.

At issue is whether the parent is obsessed with their own agenda, so that there's no space for the child to express their own will and feelings. When we take this route, we are left with no recourse other than to discipline, since to be true to herself a child can't simply follow our dictates all the time and is therefore bound to cross us. To stand up for themselves as human beings in their own right, a child needs to push back. The parenting task isn't to crush such self-assertion, but to foster it so the child becomes a full-fledged person who knows their own mind and is unafraid to express their voice, regardless of the fact it may rattle our ego and run contrary to our movie.

It's the dynamic that arises from insisting on our parental agenda that creates the need for discipline. Let me be clear what I mean when I say "agenda." I'm referring to the gamut

It's the dynamic that arises from insisting on our parental agenda that creates the need for discipline.

of our beliefs, including the ideas we cherish but aren't consciously aware of. These encompass how we define God, what it means to be a "success" in life, what makes someone beautiful, how we cope with failure, how we handle trauma, what makes a good child, what constitutes a good partner—indeed, every aspect of everyday life. Even when we aren't aware of how mired we are in our ideas of how things should be, these are always the driving force of our interactions.

The belief that a child should eat whatever we set before them is an extreme that doesn't take into account their preferences. There's no sense of parent and child in a partnership. The parent is dictator in a hierarchy. At the same time, we don't want the child to become a dictator either. At this extreme our child can eat whatever they choose, such as french fries and sundaes every day. Both extremes are unhealthy. The ideal is the middle way, whereby the parent understands that both parent and child have desires that need to be taken into account. The wise parent takes the lead, but not in a dictatorial way. Such a parent understands that unless the child's feelings are honored, lasting solutions don't emerge.

When it struck me I was interpreting Maia's refusal to eat my lasagna as an attack on my subconscious script as a gourmet chef, I was able to make a shift. Realizing my subconscious need to see myself as a mother who took the trouble to prepare gourmet food for her daughter was driving me, not what was truly best for Maia, I elected to move away from a focus on how Maia should have responded to my "great mothering" and instead express my feelings. "You know, Maia," I said, "Mommy did try to make you something you would like."

Maia responded, "I know you did, Mommy. Thank you. But next time, don't try so hard. I like all my vegetables separate, not together in a lasagna." I believe it was because I didn't put her on the defensive that she was able to acknowledge her needs in a straightforward manner. I then picked up the dish and set it aside—and with it my ego. Maia kept reading as if nothing had happened, oblivious to the battle that had been raging in my head. For her it was a simple matter of enjoying her vegetables just as they are and not about my great culinary skills, with all the emotional attachment I had to them that particular afternoon.

Strangely I felt relief. Something in me intuitively knew I had avoided a huge parenting misstep. By simply not pushing my subconscious script, I didn't attract drama. For me this was an epiphany. I realized that the idea of "discipline" is a mental construct that emerges from the parent's subconscious. What we think of as a need for discipline stems not from the child's behavior but from our emotional attachment to a particular idea of "how my child should be."

The reason we create movies of how things should be is our inability to accept ourselves, and therefore others, "as is." The key to effective parenting is to step out of the movies and into the "as is." When we embrace the "as is" of our children, we no longer blame them for not being who we need them to be, and we no longer try to change them. Our parenting moves away from control, instead becoming guidance.

Chapter 10

Abandon the Idea of Perfection

I remember the first time Maia looked at me when I yelled at her, as if to say, "Why are you looking at me like I'm a bad person?" Seeing my daughter's look of betrayal jolted me.

In that moment I became acutely aware that no child inherently feels bad. Feeling bad comes entirely from how other people interact with them, mostly their parents. The idea doesn't even occur to our children that there's something "wrong" with them until we implant it. And why do we think there's something wrong with them? Only because they are different from us.

Nancy and her daughter Samantha are an example of this, in that they have been in a clash of wills since Samantha was two years old. "Like oil and water," Nancy says of their dynamic. "I don't get her," Nancy bemoans. "She knows precisely how to push my buttons."

Is it true that Samantha is trying to push her mother's buttons? Or is what feels abrasive to Nancy simply Samantha being true to her nature? Nancy is mild mannered, orderly, and introverted; Samantha is loud, boisterous, messy, and even somewhat clumsy. In other words, Samantha's natural way of being goes against Nancy's perfectionist nature.

"I can't stop focusing on the bad things she does," Nancy complains. "Trust me, she does plenty of bad." Is Samantha truly being bad? I suggest that Nancy labels the differences she sees in her daughter as "bad" because they aren't part of her idealized image of what a daughter should be. Hence without realizing it, Nancy has fallen into the trap of disciplining her daughter simply because she is different from herself. She sees every difference between them as "bad behavior." This inevitably triggers Samantha's inbuilt survival mechanism, which causes her to be determined to assert herself even more.

An unconscious aspect of human nature involves judging and labeling those things we don't understand as "bad." We have to come to terms with the fact that at times the things children do defy logic. While some challenge our dearly held fantasies occasionally, others do so daily, even hourly. When our children's behavior falls outside our box, which is often tiny and rigid despite how we like to believe we are so open, they get judged harshly. Ironically, it's *our* brain maps that *create* the box, since children don't yet have such a box. They are flexible; we, far less so. This is especially true of children who veer off the mainstream path, have special needs, are inordinately sensitive, or have learning issues, attention problems, and so on. These children are extremely vulnerable to negative labels. Inadvertently, our unconscious use of these labels triggers in them even more behavior that's out of the norm.

Until our subconscious themes are brought to our awareness, we assume the "good" roles for ourselves and cast others in our life as "bad." This is a projection. Because we can't own up to our weaknesses, we split them off from our awareness, placing them on the other. Why do we project our weaknesses instead of owning up to them? The reason is that we haven't come to terms with our own humanness, with its capacity for grossly unconscious, even foolish error. Nor are we evolved enough to understand that the human capacity is varied, multifaceted, and unquantifiable. Just because someone falls outside the mainstream doesn't mean they are any less normal or gifted in their own right. Our rabid insistence on pushing everyone along the same bell curve has severely deleterious effects on our children, especially those who are unable to survive such normative measures.

Let's take it a step further. If your child is socially awkward and embarrasses you at a party because they aren't socially well adjusted, how do you react? You may harshly criticize and judge their behavior. This is because it feels intolerable that your progeny is different from the mainstream. You see it as a reflection of your own inadequacy, which you find unbearable.

Isn't it sad that we are unable to allow ourselves or our children to be seen in a light that's less than perfect? To be human *is* to be imperfect. Yet to admit we are imperfect is viewed as akin to a fall from grace.

If you are performing on stage in a school play and forget your lines, how do you feel? Probably so embarrassed that you wish the earth would open and swallow you. At such a moment, you torture yourself with thoughts of others laughing at you, even ridiculing you. In a ball game that's important to your team, if you drop the ball when it really matters that you catch it, how do you feel? You try to hide your embarrassment if you can, rather than simply seeing it as a dropped ball with no bearing on your character—on your inestimable value as a human being.

Embracing our imperfection is a hard lesson to integrate into our own lives, let alone teach our children. Most of us are burdened by our inability to accept our imperfection, causing our children to carry similar burdens of self-blame, self-loathing, and self-deprecation. Most women I know have issues around their looks and weight, as do many men. Others worry about being inadequate in their career. Perhaps they feel they don't make enough money. And of course we all know we have shortcomings when it comes to how we function in our relationships. Sadly parents inevitably pass on their insecurity about their failings to their children, who come to see themselves in a similar way.

Although we need to abandon our need for perfection, this doesn't mean "anything goes." We can challenge our children to do their best without demanding they become perfectionists or conform with the mainstream. I remember trying to teach Maia this through a mundane exercise in writing. Her handwriting is normally legible, even neat. But one evening when she did her homework, it was haphazard and untidy. In a gentle manner, I suggested she might rewrite the assignment in her usual tidy handwriting. Maia took umbrage: "That's so mean, Mommy. I was really trying my hardest." Tears welled up in her eyes as she added, "It hurts me that you don't like my handwriting."

Realizing I needed to guide her into an awareness that our

external acts, such as our handwriting, have no bearing on our value as people, I replied, "Thank you for sharing your feelings. You don't have to change your handwriting if you don't want to. The more important thing for you to realize is that your handwriting is not Maia. Your hair is not Maia. Your face is not Maia. Your room is not Maia. Your clothes are not Maia. Your grades are not Maia. None of these are Maia. You are more than any of this, beyond all of this. Who you are is something far more wondrous and beautiful, which is your essence. This essence can never be ugly, stupid, or inferior. It's always fine just as it is. So if I, or your teacher, or another kid tells you your hair is ugly, or your handwriting is sloppy, remember that since it's not the real you, and only a temporary way of expressing yourself, it doesn't define you. Perhaps then it won't be so hurtful anymore if I suggest you might want to write in your usual neat way. But I leave that up to you."

She looked at me dumbfounded. What on earth was Mommy talking about? I realized the concepts were hard for her to grasp, but I was sowing seeds that would bear fruit when she was ready.

Maia replied, "Okay, let me try it again. It's not such a big deal to redo it." On some level she understood that she didn't have to take these external manifestations of her personhood so seriously. She was learning to embrace her imperfections without over-dramatizing them, instead seeing them as an opportunity to learn.

When it comes to accepting ourselves as imperfect, we set the tone for our children. The degree to which they accept their imperfections tends to be the degree to which we accept and honor our own.

"Mommy, you are so fat," Maia said to me one day as she played Ride the Horse on my back. "Look at your jiggly and squishy underarms," she added. In that moment, I recognized I could either take her comments personally, allowing them to hurt me, or I could accept my anatomy just the way it is, thereby teaching her that our sense of worth doesn't need to be tied up with how we look.

Instead of telling her she was being mean and had insulted me, I responded, "Yeah, I know. Kind of like the wings of a plane, right?" We both giggled.

When a child realizes their parents are unfazed by their own imperfections, the child embraces imperfection as a fact of existence. Instead of labeling some aspects of their personality "good" and others "bad," they learn to integrate everything about them in a seamless manner.

Every child trips and tumbles innumerable times when beginning to walk. Imperfections are no different. When we accept them instead of considering them something to be ashamed of, we give them the freedom to evolve at their natural pace.

How does this work with parents who suffer from depression or self-loathing? Instead of trying to appear perfect, aren't they only too ready to admit their failings?

While most of us project a sense of lack onto the other,

> When it comes to accepting ourselves as imperfect, we set the tone for our children. The degree to which they accept their imperfections tends to be the degree to which we accept and honor our own.

creating a split between how we see ourselves and how we see the other, the depressed person creates a split within themselves. They turn their sense of lack onto themselves. Whereas most of us unleash our inner critic on someone like our children, the depressed person unleashes it on themselves. In both cases the ability to see oneself as a whole being, with strengths and imperfections, is obscured. It's only when we accept ourselves without either grandiosity or loathing—without an "I'm perfect" or "I'm hopeless" mindset—that transformation gets underway.

The "as is" of our nature needs to be accepted without qualification. The inner critic is a judgmental despot that has no value whatever. When we have compassion for ourselves instead of apologizing for who we are, we begin to accept others for who they are. Said differently, empathy for the self leads to empathy for others. In such an atmosphere, our children flourish.

When our subconscious agenda clashes with who our children inherently are, no matter what our surface intentions, it generates conflict. A child can detect when they are being coerced into an activity that isn't truly them. Therefore the intent and purpose of parental leadership must always be the natural development of the child according to the child's own unique bent. When an activity is fitted to a child's bent, the child tends to buy into it because they realize we are asking something of them that resonates with their soul.

Without giving it a thought, many fathers immediately begin buying footballs and baseball caps the moment they learn they are to have a son. They can't wait to pitch the ball for their son and teach him how to shoot baskets. But what if they have a boy who prefers ballet, as recounted in the 2000 movie Billy Elliot, in which a boy becomes torn between his passion for dance and a father who wants him to take boxing classes? Attachment to an idealized image of what a boy should be interested in made it excruciating for this father to accept his son for who he was.

Tony, a high-powered attorney, is a classic example of a father who had a hard time accepting his son. Traveling the globe, leading an action-packed life, Tony had mastered the ability to multitask to the point that efficiency had become his hallmark. His son Nathan was nothing like him. Naturally sensitive and soft-spoken, Nathan moved slowly, processed information slowly, spoke slowly. Interpreting this as resistance, even defiance, Tony was riled. Unable to understand Nathan's more dreamy, passive, observant personality, he was forever yelling at his son, "What's wrong with you? Why can't you get a move on? Hurry up, for heaven's sake." This led to Nathan shutting down and withdrawing even more.

In Tony's world, as the parent, he was right. His subconscious agenda told him life needs to be engaged with high intensity. To observe his son, who was the opposite, wreaked havoc with everything he valued. Whereas he saw Nathan's slowness as a reason for discipline, Nathan was just naturally being who he is.

As parents have expectations of sons, so too many parents hope for a daughter who will grow up to give them grandchildren. If their daughter chooses another path for herself, perhaps deciding she would rather not have children, have a variety of partners over the years, or have no partner at all, they may have great difficulty celebrating her choices.

As parents, we believe we are present for our children,

> To be present for our children means to be aware of our own subconscious agenda so we don't impose this on our children.

that we listen to them, and that we are there for them in a supportive way. Little do we realize that on countless occasions we do exactly the opposite. To be present for our children means to be aware of our own subconscious agenda so we don't impose this on our children. To listen to our children means to hear them without the obstruction of our ideas, opinions, and judgments. To be a support throughout their development means to be willing to let go of our idea of how they should live their life, which is based solely on our disposition and experience, not theirs.

In being present, listening, and supportive of our children, it's necessary to be realistic. None of us can completely free ourselves from our subconscious agenda. The key is to become aware of it, examining the ways it gets in the way of connecting with our children on the level of feelings.

Rather than punishing our children for living their own lives, we invite them to enter into self-awareness so they can shape their lives in a manner that's true to them. In this way we encourage them in their journey of becoming increasingly authentic.

Chapter 11

A Strong Child Lives Here

Because children enter the world connected to their feelings, they are aware of what makes them happy and quick to move away from what displeases them. Yet gradually, as a result of their interaction with their parents and society, they become conditioned to look not so much to their own inner being for fulfillment but to agendas that spring from their parents' and other caregivers' conditioning.

Since it's naturally quicker and easier to hand a child a ready-made script than to take the time to address a need with the kind of openness and originality called for in the moment, a parent has to be acutely aware of the tendency to impose on their child the kind of cookie-cutter solutions by which they themselves may have been raised.

Time-consuming and cumbersome as it may be to respond to our children's needs authentically, in the long-run we generate exponentially harder work for ourselves when we don't do so. This is because needs not taken care of in the moment have a way of growing out of proportion—and then they can turn rogue, resulting in seriously dysfunctional behavior. When we allow this to happen, we inadvertently dig ourselves into a pit of discontent. Which parent doesn't wish they had "done things differently" when their child was younger?

An example of how important it is to listen closely to our children—hearing what they *actually* mean and not what we *want* them to mean—comes from when my daughter was three years old and was unexpectedly bitten by a dog with which she often played. Bozo and Maia loved each other, but in the excitement of the rough-and-tumble of play, Bozo nipped her behind her ear, which required her to go to the hospital for stitches—a traumatic experience for a child of this age, not to mention for us as her parents. Between her sobs Maia passionately declared, "I hate Bozo! What's wrong with Bozo? I'm mad at him."

Afraid this incident would scar her for life and develop into a phobia of dogs, I placated her by explaining, "Oh, Maia, don't be mad. Bozo didn't mean it. He was just confused by all the excitement."

Maia was vehement: "No, Mommy, he's a mean dog. I don't like him anymore. He's bad."

In my head a commentary began running: "Oh no, damn dog. Because of him my daughter will have psychological issues around dogs for the rest of her life. She's always loved dogs, and now he's ruined everything."

About to embark on another attempt at making excuses for Bozo so Maia would see him in a better light, I caught myself. I realized my need to placate her was coming from my own anxiety. You see, I had a movie running in my head of how Maia and animals would get along, and now life had derailed my plot. The "as is" of the situation was unacceptable to me. Imagining myself the director of the movie, I had sought to manipulate Maia into my way of seeing things.

The point about feelings is that they don't have to make sense, don't need to be justified, and don't require our approval. Because we are so oriented to intellectualizing, we want to explain feelings away instead of allowing our children to simply experience them. The issue is our own discomfort, which we need to learn to tolerate.

Thankfully Maia was resolute, her expression of her feelings authentic. Accurate or not in her reasoning, she was expressing genuine outrage that Bozo had hurt her. By deflecting her feelings, I was invalidating her perception of her experience. I wanted her to feel the way I believed she should feel, not how she really felt. Had I continued down this path, I would have been the one who created a psychological problem out of the incident.

I have to give credit to my husband, who said in a matter of fact way, "These things happen and are beyond our control. Let's use this moment to teach Maia how to cope with life's traumas instead of pretending they don't happen or aren't as bad as she thinks." This was an epiphany for me, causing me to stop forcing Maia to fit in with my script and instead allowing her to feel her emotions. I actually chose to join her in her experience by allowing her to express herself vociferously.

For days Maia kept voicing her anger, even writing letters to Bozo and drawing pictures to show him how she felt. This helped her process her emotions, which gradually subsided, enabling her to welcome Bozo back into her life. My fears didn't materialize and today she continues to love dogs.

When we engage our children at their level, allowing them to follow their natural ways, words often aren't necessary. Indeed they can easily contaminate the experience. Our tuned-in presence is all that's needed. By simply witnessing our child's feelings, allowing them to sit with what they are experiencing without attempting to distract them or pressure them to move beyond their present state, we teach the art of self-reflection. I see so many children who, unsure of their own feelings, look to their parents for how they ought to feel. When a child has to constantly check with their parents to see if it's okay to feel a certain way, they have lost touch with their own center of gravity.

In my book *The Conscious Parent,* I talk about a time when Maia was four years old and in a particularly restless mood. Jumpy and hard to please, she kept saying she was bored and had nothing to do. Because this struck at my belief that I needed to be the kind of parent who keeps her child stimulated, my first instinct was to rescue her—and, in the process, myself. Isn't a good parent supposed to schedule their children's time? As I contemplated whether I should turn on the television, do a project with her, or take her to the park, the insight came to me, "How will she learn to navigate her way through her boredom if I rescue her all the time?" Our children develop emotional sturdiness when they manage their emotions without the assistance of an external aid. I told her, "It's okay to be bored. There's nothing wrong with feeling bored. Keep being bored."

She looked at me not just with great disappointment but as if I were slightly mad. As she left my room, she muttered loudly to herself and kept on muttering long after she was out of view. A little while later, I noticed her whining seemed to have abated. When I went to her room, I found her humming contentedly to her doll.

Had I not sidestepped my need to be the fixer, the rescuer, or the ever-entertaining mother, I wouldn't have been able to encourage Maia to sit with her feelings so she would learn how to navigate them on her own. Unable to tolerate the feelings Maia's boredom triggered in me (such as feeling like an inadequate mother), I would have either barked at her, told her she was being bothersome, or rescued her. In effect I would have only rescued myself, teaching her several destructive lessons in the process, such as that feelings are scary and we can't tolerate them, or that they are to be avoided and fixed through distraction. She would have learned to rely on superficial, transient aids to get her through her feelings, rather than learning to experience them in the present.

No child in touch with the present moment is going to stay bored. The present moment contains an aliveness that our children readily tap into if we allow them the space to do so instead of rushing in to fill the seeming void. This is where the parent takes the lead, as I did in this situation, setting the tone.

If a parent puts out the kind of vibes that welcome feelings, even when the feelings are difficult to tolerate, the child picks up on this, eventually learning how to manage their feelings in a healthy manner. Sadly the vibes many of us broadcast to our children indicate to them that their feelings are unwelcome, especially if they are directed toward us. In this way we undercut their ability to feel, using timeout or some other form of discipline to punish them for their feelings. As they bury their feelings even deeper, these feelings

If a parent puts out the kind of vibes that welcome feelings, even when the feelings are difficult to tolerate, the child picks up on this, eventually learning how to manage their feelings in a healthy manner.

become a hotbed for serious dysfunction in the teen years and beyond.

A child's feelings can seem silly to us as adults, but they aren't silly to the child. A case in point is fear of the dark. Eight-year old Kathleen hadn't slept through the night in weeks, as a result of which Stacey and Robert, her parents, were at a loss. A normally well-adjusted child, Kathleen had developed a fear of ghosts, zombies, and monsters that made her anxious at night. "I keep telling her there are no ghosts or zombies, but she refuses to listen to me," Stacey complained. "I'm hoarse from trying to explain that such things don't exist."

Robert added, "We've tried every trick in the book—bribing her, punishing her for waking us up, and even leaving her in her room to cry. Nothing seems to work. The child insists on being terrified."

Losing patience with their daughter, Kathleen's parents were beginning to think she was behaving abnormally for a girl her age and suggested maybe they needed a psychological evaluation to see if she was hallucinating.

"The first step is to understand that anxieties aren't a disciplinary matter," I told them. "The second is to stop insisting there are no zombies or ghosts."

"What?" Stacey protested. "I can't encourage my child to

think there are weird creatures in the world! I don't want her friends to laugh at her."

"You let her believe in Santa Claus, didn't you?" I pressed.

"Of course," Kathleen retorted, "because Santa is benign, not creepy and scary."

"When our children express their fears, we need to align with them, not resist them," I explained. "When we resist them, their fears get blown out of proportion because now our children feel alone in their anxiety."

To react to the anxieties our children experience by bribing, threatening, or punishing them fails to address what their fears represent to them. Through imaginary symbols such as ghosts, zombies, and monsters, our children are trying to show us they feel unsafe and ill-equipped to handle a scary world. They are asking us to help them make sense of how they fit into a frightening scenario and to give them tools to do so. When we tell them there are no monsters, we contradict what they are feeling. To them their fears are monsters, which is why they "see" these fears as images— not unlike the images in our dreams at night as adults.

"Kathleen is expressing something very real to her, begging you to understand her," I continued. "What she's trying to tell you is that she feels unsafe. She's expressing a lack of control in her life. Instead of telling her ghosts don't exist, help her feel powerful in her relationship with the world."

"How do we do that?" Roger asked.

I explained that there are many ways to create a sense of safety for a child, but the foundation is to allow them to feel what they are feeling. Validation and empathy are key. I've helped many children create safe zones in their rooms where they pick soft toys to protect them at night. Some children put posters on their windows announcing, "No Ghosts Allowed Here" or "Strong Child Lives Here—Back Off."

A friend of mine, today one of the strongest people I know, used to sleep with about a dozen soft-toy animals lined up on his pillow, to the point that his father once asked, "And where does your head fit?"

With one child, we watched the movie E.T., which enabled him to see that aliens and monsters can have huge hearts. We focused on how something may look scary on the outside but could be caring and loving on the inside.

With a slightly older child, we role-played zombies and monsters, which allowed him to give his fears a voice and form. As someone shared with me, "I did stories with my daughters. We talked about how silly ghosts were and that they can't be that powerful. Heck, the only place they seem to live is crappy houses, they can't come out during the day, and what are they really going to do? Go through me? Ooooh, so scary."

Another child wrote letters to her secret fairy and asked for protection. Every night, her mother in the guise of the fairy left notes under her pillow. Through these beautiful exchanges, the child learned to trust that the world is a safe place.

There are all kinds of ways we can help our children cope with their world. Creativity is what's needed, not admonishment or discipline. When we empower our children in this way, we enable them to deal with stress, thereby equipping them for a lifetime of meeting trauma with resilience instead of fear. How we help them when they are young is how they will later survive adult crises.

Kathleen began to role-play scenarios in therapy, assigning

us alternating roles as different creatures for different scenes. She also used figurines to create an army to protect her in the "battle against the monsters." In time she gained mastery over her fears, learning to navigate the onslaught of ghosts, zombies, and monsters when she faced them at night. In other words, the work she did with her parents in therapy helped empower her when she was alone in the dark.

There are all kinds of ways we can help our children cope with their world. Creativity is what's needed, not admonishment or discipline.

When a child is allowed to feel exactly what they are feeling while receiving support from us, the feelings become integrated instead of split off. Feelings never go away when they aren't allowed to be what they are, but morph into a distorted form that can manifest in aberrant behavior. In other words, feelings that are denied have a way of metastasizing, becoming emotionally cancerous. Now they show up elsewhere, perhaps in disruption of sleep, nightmares, physical problems such as stomach aches or headaches—and, in more extreme situations, as acting out or even depression.

As I've emphasized several times now, feelings left unprocessed develop into unmet needs that can wreak havoc later. The prudent parent allows their child's feelings to be fully metabolized.

Chapter 12

It's Not about You

Every parent thinks they are raising their child in a manner that's best for the child. After all, who of us doesn't believe we should put our children's needs first, even ahead of our own?

Though this is what we tell ourselves, I propose it's a delusion. The reality is that all of us function from our *own* needs—including when it comes to the way we raise our children.

I often ask groups of parents why they had children. Their answers include: I wanted to experience what it was like, I love children, I wanted to become a parent, I wanted a family, I wanted to feel what it's like to love a child and be loved by that child. These are actual answers I've received many times.

What stands out from these answers is the word "I." This indicates that for many of us, having children is more about us than it is about the child. It's something we grow up believing we are expected to do. Almost like an item on a checklist that includes education, career, purchasing a home, to have a child allows us to feel "normal." We associate it with leading a successful life.

Our children fill an emotional need for us. Each of us comes with a longing to be loved unconditionally by another. Often this is the driving force behind wanting to have children. As part of our desire to feel complete, we tend to use our children to fulfill our unfulfilled dreams, pushing them to achieve as if this could somehow fill our longing. Preoccupied with our own needs in this way, we can easily fail to honor our child's needs.

Paradoxically, preoccupation with our own needs can also have the opposite effect. Instead of failing to hear our children's feelings, we become overly sensitive to their feelings. When this happens, we are likely to go to enormous lengths to shield them. The "helicopter" parent is a classic example of what I'm referring to. This parent feels a need to hover over their children 24/7, believing they are being a conscientious mother or father. Many such parents sacrifice all their free time, interests, and energy to be with their children around the clock. Though they appear to be selfless, such parents are in reality needy.

In my parents' generation, a child's feelings were frequently overridden. In our more psychologically attuned era there's a tendency to overprotect. This happens when we confuse being attuned to our children with becoming overly identified with what they are going through.

For instance, one parent said to me, "I had a scary experience with one of my teachers in elementary school. Ever since, I've harbored a fear of authority figures. I didn't realize I had this fear because it was buried. Almost thirty years later, when my own eight-year-old daughter was given a bit of a talking to by her teacher, I felt those old feelings well up in me as I remembered my own pain, which resulted in me crying harder than she was crying. When I told her we would change schools, she was shocked and began soothing me instead of the other way around. 'I don't want to change schools or my teacher,' she explained. 'I like my teacher. I just don't like that she talked to me that way. It's okay, Mommy. I will be okay.'"

Learning to walk the fine line between being attuned to our children and overreacting is an art. It requires the parent to become aware of how their own neediness may be in operation at any given moment. You might wonder, "How can I be needy when all I do is give? How can sitting at a tennis court hour after hour, watching my child play, sacrificing my weekends, and paying armloads be about my need?" To understand how we use our children to fulfill our unmet expectations requires us to enter an honest process of self-reflection, which is what I ask parents to do in *The Conscious Parent*.

To honor our children's feelings requires us to grow ourselves up, even as we help our children cross their developmental hurdles. I still remember complaining to my mother when Maia was young, "She's being impossible. I don't understand her." Because I was unable to recognize where my daughter was coming from, she was driving me crazy, which of course caused me to project my frustrations onto her. The result was that I was being short with her. Observing this, my mother was initially patient with me, allowing me to feel upset that Maia wasn't following my fantasy of who she should be. However, there came a day when, after a particularly harrowing morning, my mother sat me down and said, "You better snap out of your sense of victimhood. You aren't the victim here. If anyone is, it's Maia. She isn't to blame for the fact you can't understand her, and neither is it her fault you've never encountered a child like her before. She's just being herself. It's your responsibility to figure her out and deal with whoever she wants to be in any given moment."

Our children didn't come into the world to be our puppets. They came here to struggle, fumble, thrive, and enjoy—a journey for which they need our encouragement. Neither are our children here to purposely defy us. In their natural state, they intend neither to comply nor defy (though they are preprogrammed to mimic). Both compliance and defiance are indicators that parenting has gone awry. To put things back on course, we need to embrace our children exactly as they are.

Many of us have never learned how to tolerate feelings, whether intense pleasure or distress. Instead we sidestep an authentic connection with whatever is happening at this moment, right now. Hence we have mothers who say, "Oh, you are feeling sad. Let me get you a bowl of ice cream." The mother is trying to be a good mother, but she's sidestepping the real issue. To allow her child to feel sad is hard for her because she can't stand to see her child in pain.

When we unconsciously insert ourselves into an equation in which we don't belong, we interfere with our children's ability to engage with life's ebb and flow in an organic manner. We

> Our children didn't come into the world to be our puppets. They came here to struggle, fumble, thrive, and enjoy—a journey for which they need our encouragement.

impede the natural development of their resourcefulness. For instance, when Sheila's twelve-year-old daughter Maria complained she hadn't been invited to a friend's bat mitzvah celebration, the mother couldn't bear to see her daughter's disappointment. Picking up the phone, she called the girl's mother, who was a participant in her book club, and requested Maria be included. The mother was incensed that Sheila had the audacity to make such a request and began blacklisting her as well as her daughter.

When Sheila came to me outraged at this mother, ready to go to war with her, I pointed out that none of this would have happened had she simply tolerated her daughter's discomfort. To be excluded is a normal life experience that everyone needs to be able to cope with and not feel inferior. Over-identification with her daughter caused Sheila to deprive Maria of one of life's normal experiences, short-circuiting a chance for her to discover her resilience and thereby robbing her of the opportunity to develop a skill that's vital in life.

The real issue was that Sheila was struggling with her own feelings of inferiority in social settings. Maria's disappointment created such anxiety for Sheila that she tried to manipulate her daughter's social world. In effect she was saying to Maria, "You aren't capable of handling this. I will take over and manage it." In a subtle way, she was putting Maria in her place. The silent message was, "If you can't get yourself invited to celebrations that reflect well on me, I will have to step in to ensure that our family receives its due recognition." Of course, at a deeper level, Sheila was tapping into her own sense of being rejected as a child, which is what was driving her preoccupation with her family's social image.

Whereas a parent like Sheila jumps in and rescues her

child at the slightest indication of pain, a parent who has suffered years of trauma may handle the situation by telling their child to "toughen up." I think of Madeline, a mother in her fifties, whose parents had been emotionally unavailable to her during many disruptions such as leaving for overseas jobs, living with relatives, a divorce, and so on. As a parent, she found herself unable to relate to her children's feelings because the issues seemed trivial compared with what she had gone through.

For instance, on one occasion her daughter came home feeling bad because she wasn't assigned the lead role in a school play for which she had worked really hard. Despite the girl's tears, her mother was unable to empathize and retorted, "What? You're crying over such a little thing? Do you have any idea what I went through in my life? I would never let something so minor bother me. Get over it." Withdrawing to her room, the daughter cried even more, distancing herself from her mother for days.

When Madeline relayed the incident to me, she said, "I thought I was helping her to cope and be strong by teaching her to ride the waves of life and not get crushed."

I explained, "You're measuring your daughter's experience against your own. Because you were left to deal with such huge adult-like problems at a young age, without the chance to process your feelings, you are out of touch with how it feels to be vulnerable. You impose the way you handled your life onto your daughter, but she isn't you. You've worked hard to ensure she doesn't experience your hardships, while on another level you scorn her for feeling those hardships she deems real. Just because they aren't real for you doesn't mean they aren't real for her."

Having pointed out that Madeline was reacting to her child's sadness based on her own experiences in comparison, I want to acknowledge that her desire to see her child become resilient was well intentioned. The issue is that we have to start where the child is, not with where we believe the child ought to be. This is when therapy can be helpful, since a skilled therapist can facilitate the processing of a client's feelings rather than imposing their own agenda on those feelings in the way parents tend to.

If Madeline had first sat with her child, allowing her daughter to experience her feelings just the way they were, she could then have gently led her into an understanding of the fact we don't always get what we want. Through her tolerance of her child's emotions, she would have shown her how to negotiate the inevitable ups and downs of everyday life.

Chapter 13

Learn to Read
Your Child's Cues

Our children are constantly telling us what's going on in their inner world through their behavior. But if we don't know how to decipher the clues, we can't get to the root of the behavior and therefore can't offer the guidance and support that's needed.

For instance, a client's teen refused to bathe. His room was a disaster and he left a trail of chaos everywhere he went in the house. Unable to see beyond the behavior to the underlying message in the behavior, his mother berated him daily about his slovenly ways. She felt her only recourse was to punish him. First she took away his cell phone, then his computer, followed by his Play Station. When none of these worked, she grounded him, which only served to increase her misery since he messed up the home more than ever. Finally exasperated, she slapped him and screamed, "I wish you had never been born!" At this point she realized the situation was out of control and they needed professional help.

In therapy I explained to the mother that no child truly

wants to smell, live in a pigsty, and behave in an ugly manner. If you watch little children before we impose our agenda on them, you see how proud they are of their lives. They are proud of a simple drawing they made, proud of being able to dress themselves, proud of being able to tie their own shoes, as well as proud of their new toy, new shoes, or new clothes. If a child behaves in a manner that shows they have no personal pride, it means their internal world has very possibly become a depressing place to live. When their internal sense of themselves is so impoverished, this feeling can't help but spill over into their external reality.

The mother began to see that her son's behavior was less an act of defiance and more an indication of his inner chaos. Once she realized this, she became his ally in his pain instead of his adversary. She stopped focusing on whether he had cleaned his room and instead turned her attention to why he wasn't motivated to be tidy.

As the mother's emphasis shifted from fixing her son's behavior to helping him with his low self-esteem, their home became a safe place for the son to be transparent. Instead of nagging about all the things he hadn't done, the mother forged a connection with her son by spending time with him, even if it was to play video games she ordinarily never engaged in. She also went for walks with him and took him to lunch. Slowly he came out of his shell to the point he could talk about what was bothering him. Therapy helped them both open up about the ways they had hurt each other in the past. As the son began to share his feelings more, his negativity lightened. Although the process took almost a year, by the end he had begun to take care of himself and had found a full-time job.

This approach isn't quick. But because it's real instead of artificial, it yields lasting results. By focusing on the unearthing of a child's potential within a safe and nurturing environment, we honor the fact that every child holds within them the wisdom required for their own growth. Who knew that parenting involves sleuthing for clues that reveal what's being said through a child's behavior?

Having said this, I would be the first to admit that since children don't use logic or intellectual theories to explain how they feel, it can be challenging for a parent to understand the meaning behind their actions. Most of us don't even understand our own actions, so how can we understand those of another?

As adults, many of us have adopted highly dysfunctional means of expressing our pain. For example, when we feel hurt, we may go to a bar and drink all night instead of expressing the pain we are experiencing in an articulate way. Or we may lash out at our spouse by sleeping with someone else. But can younger children get in the car and head to a bar? Can they take $1,000 and go to the casino?

Children have similar struggles with feeling hurt, except they cover up their hurt by rolling their eyes, using rude words, or sticking their tongue out at us. As the stakes become higher, they engage in more risky behavior, which is why you see young teens taking drugs, binge drinking, or being promiscuous. These are children who are screaming for help but not receiving it.

When you can read the subtext of behavior and recognize what the surface acting out is truly about, you realize that dysfunctional behavior comes about incrementally. The girl who suddenly runs away from home, ending up on the street, didn't get to this state overnight. The state she's now in has been built up slowly over the years from her countless unhelpful moment-to-moment interactions with her parents.

As an indicator of how difficult it can initially be to identify what a child is feeling, parents often ask me, "How am I supposed to know what my child is feeling when he keeps sticking his tongue out at me in defiance?" The parent is so focused on the fact the child is sticking his tongue out that they don't even consider the underlying factors. I tell such parents that while their child may be expressing disrespect on one level, this is superficial. I also caution them that if they respond at this level, they will perpetuate the behavior.

The parent then counters, "But when he sticks out his tongue, aren't I supposed to reprimand him? Isn't that what any normal parent would do?"

"You may be able to get him to stop sticking out his tongue with discipline," I explain. "However, because the underlying cause isn't being addressed, your child will just turn to another form of acting out. Until you discover the reason for the behavior, it will keep mutating."

To help this mother understand how the behavior her son is exhibiting originated, I explain, "You started your interaction with your son with a subconscious script—you just weren't aware you did this. Your script said your instructions needed to be followed. If they weren't, you saw it as an act of defiance. While you can argue your instructions were legitimate, the fact is your son didn't buy into them. This is where the disconnect lies. When you realized your subconscious script wasn't being fulfilled, you likely reacted to your son with anger, perhaps also with put downs, and no doubt at times more subtly with a vibe of disappointment.

As he picked up on this, he began to push back. Of course, this fueled your frustration even more. The cycle, which began when your movie wasn't working out in everyday life, became self-perpetuating."

The mother looks at me astonished. It's clear she's hearing what's being said. I continue, "The reality is that the more you punish your son, the more he'll resist you. The only way to stop this madness is to understand that your son doesn't buy into what you are asking of him because he has begun tuning you out, since he feels chores are more important to you than he is. This doesn't mean he doesn't need to do the chores. It does mean you must first reconnect with him so he feels engaged with you and therefore values what you are asking of him. He needs to see his chores as a valid contribution on his part and not simply an imposition on your part because you are in control. It's your job to help him recognize the importance of the contribution he makes."

It's understandable that we believe a child's reaction is related to asking them to do a simple chore. What we don't realize is that the child isn't even paying attention to what we are asking but is reacting to our energy. It's happening on a feeling level, not on the surface level of tidying their room or putting the dishes up.

"So what do I do when he's disrespectful?" the mother asks.

"For now stop focusing on his defiance or his negative behavior. Act like they don't exist, letting them blow right past you without touching you. Instead, direct your attention to the fact he's hurting from his perception that he's lost connection with you. Touch the hurt at its depths. Only when you do this does it become possible to address the

Whenever we lose it with our children, it's because our own pain has resurfaced.

external behavior without having it morph into some other dysfunction."

"That's ironic," says the mother, "because every time he's rude to me, *I* feel like the hurt child."

"Exactly," I agree. "Each time our subconscious agenda doesn't get met, we enter the space of a hurt child. Because our hurt self wasn't healed when we were children, if someone reawakens this hurt within us, we erupt. This is why our children can trigger such fury in us."

Whenever we lose it with our children, it's because our own pain has resurfaced. Usually this pain originates from before age ten, when we felt out of control and helpless in many ways. Trying to gain control, our adult self flails about wildly in an effort to stave off the feeling of vulnerability that's been awakened. What we could never do as a child, we now do as an adult. The tragedy is that we are unleashing our pent-up frustration on the wrong person. Instead of our parents, our children now become the punching bag. This is how the same patterns of behavior reoccur in families over generations.

To the degree we unearth and face our residual pain from childhood, we will be able to discern our children's true feelings and identify a wise course of action that honors those feelings.

Chapter 14

What It Means
to Honor Your Child

When we enter the parenting journey with an understanding of the importance of connecting to our children's
feelings and creating an open space for their authentic voice
to be heard, we experience a different energy toward them.
Dictatorial, controlling parenting now shifts to a partnership with our children, which means we honor their feelings
and therefore fully consider their needs.

To honor feelings is to embrace the fact that feelings
underpin everything we do. As we have been seeing, actions
are an ongoing expression of feelings. So if we want to see
a change in our child's behavior, we need to start with how
our child feels.

Since it's a rule of thumb that all negative behavior is a
manifestation of hurt feelings, parents often misunderstand
this to mean they need to give into their children's feelings,
which can seduce parents into becoming permissive. This
isn't what I mean. To honor a child's feelings doesn't mean
we capitulate to their wishes. It isn't about either agreeing

or disagreeing with our child. It's a mistake to imagine we need to agree or disagree, since to do so is always from the vantage of our agenda. Whenever we measure our child's behavior against our agenda, we ride roughshod over their uniqueness and thereby dishonor them.

Honoring feelings is about being aligned with our child's holistic development, not necessarily with their whims at a particular moment. To discern whether you are honoring feelings, ask yourself: What does my child need from me at this moment to thrive? Does my child need me to say "yes" or to say "no?" What will allow my child to develop self-awareness and self-regulation?

For this approach to work, we have to be able to distinguish between our own emotional baggage from childhood and what our insight tells us our child needs. Such a discernment demands the same level of sleuthing it takes to discover our children's true feelings. Just as we have to find out what they are feeling that's driving their behavior, we have to identify our own real feelings.

A conversation with a client called Michele, a mother of three who was having a hard time connecting with her children, illustrates how it can take a little digging to identify what we are feeling and separate it from what our child requires. A physics professor at the local university, she was accustomed to logic and theory, which meant her children's chaotic ways confounded her. In this particular

> **Whenever we measure our child's behavior against our agenda, we ride roughshod over their uniqueness and thereby dishonor them.**

therapy session, she expressed she was having an especially hard time with her oldest daughter. "She's breaking all my rules," she complained. "I'm at my wits' end. She's moody, defiant, and constantly in my face. I feel like slapping her."

"That's not a feeling," I interjected.

Michele looked startled.

"How does she make you *feel*?" I asked.

Michele came back instantly, "I feel like screaming."

"That's still not a feeling; it's an emotional reaction. You want to scream because she's making you feel a certain way. What is that feeling?"

Puzzled, Michele was silent for several moments before saying in a subdued tone, "I feel really, really helpless."

"There you go," I said. "Now you are getting to the root of your reactions. How old does she make you feel?"

"About three."

"So when your daughter is disrespectful of you, your three-year-old self is triggered."

"Yes. And because it feels horrible, I now want to be horrible to her."

"Payback—our most commonly used parenting strategy," I said. Then I added, "Of course, the reason she's being disrespectful is she feels you've been horrible to her."

The feelings Michele herself had experienced at three years of age were resurfacing in her relationship with her daughter, blocking her ability to see what her daughter needed. Thus she was inadvertently fueling conflict in their relationship.

Once Michele understood how her past pain was resurfacing, she realized her task was twofold. First, it was to move away from fixing her daughter's surface behavior. Second, she needed to heed the cry for help hidden in this behavior.

In other words, precisely at the point where it appears that our children are trying to exclude us from their lives, defy us, or manipulate us, they are signaling they need us. If we don't heed the call, they will split these valuable feelings off, only to later either dump them on their own adult self through self-sabotage or on their children and grandchildren.

With our children's emotional growth in mind, the need to be either authoritarian or permissive fades away. We begin to see that parenting needn't be about a strategy or technique. Instead it's an approach to everyday life that allows us to relate organically to the child's behavior in its as-is form, on the spot, constantly attuned to the natural rhythm of the child.

I remember when every time I asked my daughter to show me her homework, she would snap, "I can do it Mommy, really. Please leave me alone." My reaction was outrage. How obnoxious and rude! I was trying to help, but she was shooing me away. Every evening at homework time the struggle continued. I would complain to my husband, "Look how she talks to me, always barking at me, in a bad mood. I just don't understand it."

It was then that I realized I had to change the way I interpreted my daughter's behavior if the situation was going to improve. Instead of viewing her rudeness as a problem, I tried to uncover what she was trying to tell me. What part did I play in generating her reaction? I came to see that she was acting the way she was because she felt micromanaged by me, overwhelmed by my need to control every detail of her homework. This wasn't at all what she needed. On the contrary, she required space, autonomy, and my trust.

As this insight dawned on me, instead of thinking of myself as the innocent party, I accepted that I was behaving in the very ways I had thought *she* was behaving. I, not her, was the one being rude and obnoxious in my invasion of her space, contaminating it with my subconscious agenda. Once I realized this, I became involved with her homework only when she asked for help. The result was that her rudeness dissipated, the house became calmer, and I was free to do my own thing.

The only way parents can honor their children's feelings is by first honoring their own. Only when we are out of touch with our own feelings, divorced from our spirit, are we unable to enter the feeling world of our children.

Honoring our children is about treating them as real people, just as we ourselves long to be treated, though in an age-appropriate manner. The consequence of this is that—other than issues of safety, when the parent is required to be resolute—most parenting will occur in grey areas that involve both the child's and the parent's personal feelings about an issue. Our ability to live in the grey instead of resorting to either black or white determines how well we honor both our child's and our own feelings.

To live in the grey requires differentiating between true feelings and our emotional reactions. They are vastly different. A feeling comes from the heart and is a response to what's arising in the moment. An emotional reaction is a programmed knee-jerk from our subconscious patterns of our past. For the most part, we operate in reaction mode, so that our emotions eclipse both our child's and our own authentic feelings. This is why we have so many problems with our children.

To honor our child's feelings is bedrock to effective parenting because it's where connection is established.

To honor our child's feelings is bedrock to effective parenting because it's where connection is established. If a child doesn't feel connected to us, our presence in their space immediately generates tension in them. They don't see us as a partner and don't sense we've come into their room in the spirit of an alliance. To them it feels like the two of us are worlds apart. Because they experience no meaningful connection with us, when we ask them to do a chore, it's as if they are being ordered to do something by a drill sergeant—or worse, an enemy. This is why they either ignore our instructions or, if pressed enough, retaliate. When we react by punishing them, it reinforces their perception of us as their adversary, which results in increased hostility toward us.

Chapter 15

Is What You Are Asking Fair?

A client of mine who had to go out late one night left her seven-year-old in his room at 10:30 at night while the nanny slept in another room. She told the child to turn the television off after thirty minutes and go to sleep. When she returned two hours later, her child was still awake and watching TV. "What's wrong with you?" she yelled. "You disobeyed me, so you won't be allowed any more TV for a week."

The bewildered child wailed, "I lost track of time. I didn't know thirty minutes had passed." Since the mother looked at the situation from an adult mindset, she thought he was lying. How could someone forget such a simple instruction? Realizing he was going to be deprived of his favorite programs for the next seven days, the boy went to sleep sobbing.

This mother did what she thought best. She believed it was her duty to discipline her son by depriving him of something he liked. She felt that going without television for a week would teach him respect for her rules. Little did she realize she had accomplished none of this.

Even less did she realize she had created the entire situation by setting her son up for failure. Children at seven years of age are mostly developmentally incapable of managing their time. Had this mother understood this, she would have devised safeguards for success, such as setting an alarm clock or calling her son, rather than holding onto an unrealistic expectation of how mature and responsible he was. What this mother categorized as "defiance" was nothing of the kind. Her son was simply being what seven-year-olds are—unaware of time.

Instead of teaching her son respect, the incident confused and shamed him, which resulted in a decreased sense of connection with his mother. More tragically, he felt belittled, which had the effect of causing him to believe he was incompetent. He had failed his mother—all because he had been given a responsibility that was inappropriate for his age. He may not remember when to shut the TV off, but he certainly would remember his mother's anger for years to come because her reaction had created an *emotional imprinting*.

Age appropriateness is a keystone of effective parenting. We do our children a disservice by putting them in situations they aren't yet mature enough to handle.

I think of a toddler who pitched a fit in the supermarket. The parent, unable to calm the child, threatened to spank her. When the child continued to scream, the parent marched her to the restroom and thrashed her.

In therapy with me the mother exclaimed, "Dammit. Why does she always act out when I'm the busiest, such as when I'm shopping?" (Of course, this is when we show the least patience and empathy, and are most tense.)

I explained that the toddler may have pitched a fit for a

variety of reasons and that it was important to understand what these might be. Was the toddler tired, hungry, distracted, or in need of something? Whatever the precise cause, it wasn't that the toddler was being purposefully difficult, which is what the mother assumed. Toddlers all over the world get punished for things that are simply out of their control. Instead of disciplining her child, the mother needed to move away from her agenda and focus on the toddler's needs, since an adult is capable of infinitely greater flexibility than a toddler.

> Age appropriateness is a keystone of effective parenting. We do our children a disservice by putting them in situations they aren't yet mature enough to handle.

In such a situation, don't try to reason with the child and certainly don't punish. Instead you might pick up the toddler and leave the supermarket. This is the *natural* consequence of such a situation—and it applies even if the child is screaming for a toy or candy. Wanting a treat isn't evil and therefore doesn't require punishment.

Parents need to understand that toddlers are by nature unpredictable, emotional, and impulsive. Their brain—and therefore their ability to regulate their impulses—simply hasn't developed fully enough to modulate their response to the level of stimulation they encounter in a store.

It's right here, at ages one and two, that many children begin to shut down their inquisitiveness as they are slapped or yelled at for reaching out for something on a store shelf that they want to explore. For them, the vast array of items in a store is an invitation to fulfill their desire to learn about their world. When we stifle this, is it any wonder we end up with a child who isn't interested in learning at school, let alone doing homework?

One evening a friend was in a Chinese restaurant around nine o'clock when, at the table opposite, a baby began crying. The mother became visibly distraught when she was unable to quiet the child, given that her parents were urging her to "take the child to the restroom and give him a good spanking to show him who's in charge." My friend stepped over to the table and suggested the mother take her baby next door to a supermarket, placing him over her shoulder and walking the aisles in a relaxed manner. The mother took my friend's advice. When he later left the restaurant, the child was sleeping in the mother's arms.

In the above situation, it's true the mother's precious time with her parents was cut short. Someone who wishes to be a parent needs to anticipate that such situations are at times to be expected when they have a young child. Although our agenda as a parent may be to have dinner with our parents, our child's agenda has to take precedence. It may also help to go for dinner early in the evening, when the child is interested in either eating or playing with the food, instead of at nine o'clock at night, when most babies and toddlers are sleeping.

Despite the best of planning, there will inevitably be times when we are situation-bound and can't simply leave. When we have tried calming, distracting, entertaining, and feeding a child, and nothing works, we have no option but to tolerate the toddler's cries. A flight on a plane is an example. The parent has to accept that responding kindly to the child is of far higher priority than punishing the child because of the frowns of other passengers. This is a situation in which we have to just grin and bear it.

In all situations of age inappropriateness, the onus is on the parent to accommodate to the situation, not on the child. When children are older, they can enter a partnership with their parent, whereby they are asked to take responsibility for their actions. But in the case of a toddler, we need to remember that the toddler didn't create these rigid parameters and therefore shouldn't be made to suffer for them.

There's another aspect of age-appropriateness that can be enormously helpful to parents. Before a child matures to a certain level, they are bound to behave in childish ways—it's natural for their age. When such behavior occurs, it's important not to turn it into an issue. I find that in such situations a sense of humor is an age-appropriate response.

Nothing breaks up tension and ends conflict more effectively than laughter. For this reason I inject humor into my parenting whenever possible. For instance, if Maia is in a surly mood and barks at me instead of speaking respectfully, rather than reacting to her I sing, "Ms. Barker is in the house, Ms. Barker is in the house." Inevitably she breaks into a giggle.

Similarly, when I inadvertently yell at her and catch myself, I make fun of myself by saying, "Gosh, I can really yell, can't I? I bet I yell louder than you. Come on, let's see who yells louder." Then we

In all situations of age inappropriateness, the onus is on the parent to accommodate to the situation, not on the child.

have a yelling match, which causes us to forget why I was yelling in the first place.

When we parent from a state of abundance and wholeness in this way, instead of with strictness, we send out vibes of comfort and ease with our imperfections. This is a vital lesson to pass on to our children, as they will mirror the fact we are okay with being less-than-mature.

Regarding immature behavior in this lighter way also mitigates a child's anxiety, as the growing child realizes that the ability to accept their current level of development is a quality to be coveted, not to be ashamed of. There's a realization that at different ages we spontaneously act in ways appropriate for that age. Little boys and girls simply aren't meant to be "little gentlemen and ladies."

Embracing age-appropriateness as our children develop has an unexpected plus. When they get to be teenagers and find a good friend is suddenly best friends with someone else, or they "fall in love" and the relationship doesn't last, they realize these are natural occurrences at this age and not the end of the world. In other words, a child whose behavior at the different stages of development has been totally acceptable to their parent becomes a teen who can survive the excruciating pain of a breakup without completely falling to pieces, or tolerate getting a C on a test without resorting to medication, knowing that in the right time their love life and their career will come together in a way that's just right for them.

Chapter 16

How to Stay Sane as Your Child Goes Through Phases

All parents inevitably go through periods of turmoil when raising a child, at times experiencing severe disruption to their schedules. Nights when a child's sleep is disrupted by such incidents as bed-wetting, sleepwalking, and nightmares are par for the course. Granted it can be exhausting to wake up several times a night to attend to a child or to have to change bed linen. The mistake is to turn these into disciplinary issues instead of recognizing them as natural moments of upheaval. If we see such times as normal instead of telling ourselves our child is being "bad," the issue becomes one of tolerating the anxiety and frustration these phases in a child's development trigger for us.

Instead of clamping down on our children in such periods of turbulence, our task is to calm and center ourselves so we are able to ride the waves associated with bringing up a child. There are multiple peaks and troughs a parent simply has to navigate without labeling them "good" or "bad."

In the case of sleep, most of the time it's natural for a child to fall asleep when tired. We can see this with babies and infants, who don't lie awake complaining they "can't go to sleep." They go to sleep when they are sufficiently tired. If a child fights sleep at a certain age, this is one of those phases the parent has to tolerate. With a very young child, patience is all that's required. When the child becomes a little older, we can make sure we avoid overstimulating the child when nap time or bedtime are approaching, helping them tune into their natural sleep rhythm. On this note, it's helpful to be aware that the light from a television or a computer works against this natural rhythm. By learning to be practical about these matters, we pass through such phases without doing psychological damage to our child.

Learning to tolerate the discomfort that at times arises around issues of sleep, food, grades, and so on, allows our children the space to sort these things out for themselves. Children are naturally resourceful and only require our guidance, not our manipulation. In this way they become self-regulating. In contrast, when we manipulate, we end up with children who can't self-regulate and who therefore in turn manipulate us by lying, cheating, sabotaging their potential with drugs or excessive alcohol use, or becoming utterly apathetic, not caring about anything.

Children are naturally resourceful and only require our guidance, not our manipulation.

I have seen firsthand the damaging effects of turning natural developmental issues into a cause for discipline. One particular couple came to me at their wits' end. Exhausted to the point of being bleary eyed, they hadn't enjoyed a sound night's sleep for months because their two-year-old son kept coming to their bed at night. Reaching boiling point, these parents first locked him in his room, leaving him to scream for hours. Completely frustrated when this didn't work, they took an even more extreme measure, locking him outside the house in the cold in his pajamas. Let me stress that these weren't bad people, but parents who were simply out of answers.

I suggested that refusing to sleep in his own bed was a sign the child either needed more connection with his parents or greater autonomy. As we talked, it became apparent that the subconscious script these parents were operating from was rooted in their own anxiety, which caused them to be ambivalent in how they related to their son. During the day they were overprotective of him, helicoptering his every move, which fostered dependence. At night, since the child experienced separation anxiety when he wasn't allowed to sleep in their bed, they had to suffer the consequences of this dependence. Changing the rules on their son—being overprotective all day, then abandoning him at night—triggered panic in him.

Once we understood what the child was communicating through his screaming, we worked out a way for the parents to let go of their overprotectiveness incrementally. As this took effect in the various everyday aspects of the child's life, the normal ability to sleep alone naturally followed. The parents simply had to be patient while the switch, which was inevitably turbulent for a time, took effect.

Again, this wasn't the disciplinary issue the parents imagined it to be. It was a dysfunction rooted in their way of relating to their son, which was being driven by their own subconscious needs. In this case the child required greater autonomy so he could stand on his own two feet. In other cases a child may need just the opposite—increased connection with a parent who might be gone all day or is emotionally unavailable. Such a child may cry out for the parent's presence, only in this case the child is communicating a lack of connection rather than a neediness fueled by dependency. The parent needs to decipher the real message.

Some parents don't like to have their child in their bed at all; other parents allow the child in their bed long past an appropriate age. A child who is still sleeping in their parent's bed when they are emotionally capable of sleeping in their own bed is a sure sign of a parent subverting their child's normal development. Such enmeshment is driven by the parent's subconscious need to be dependent on the child or to keep the child dependent on them so they feel needed as a parent. This is unhealthy and detrimental to the child's progression toward autonomy. It happens when parents are unaware of their own unmet needs and use their children to assuage their inner longing.

A parent's essential oneness with their child is different from the symbiosis in which their relationship begins. But if oneness and symbiosis are confused, as they often are, the result is the symbiosis continues long beyond an age when it's beneficial to the child.

Symbiosis is a state in which a child is utterly dependent on the parent, as if the parent were a part of the child. Symbiosis is necessary at first because the only way a child can get their needs met is through the parent. While this is appropriate early in the child's life, it's crucial the parent encourage the child to form their own unique identity at an appropriate pace. If the symbiosis continues too long, the child fails to develop an independent sense of self and remains needy into the adult years. Such neediness then sabotages the individual's ability to function well in the adult world.

Notice I said the parent needs to "encourage" the child to form their own identity, not force. Too often we either hurry a child's development or retard it by interfering with the child's growing desire for autonomy. It's crucial that the child set the timetable, supported by the parent. Be aware that this process isn't linear, like a sloped line on a graph. It will bounce all over the place as it gradually becomes habit. This will lead to increasing independence on the child's part, ending the symbiosis in which the child's life began. Whereas the parent's oneness with a child needs to continue, the symbiosis needs to taper off and in due course end. Tragically, in all too many homes this natural process of ending the symbiosis is thwarted by the parent's own neediness, so that the parent's identity is entangled with how their child performs. Grades, sports, hobbies, the way the child dresses, the child's behavior—everything becomes a statement about the parent.

The desire to control another comes from a mistaken view of symbiosis, wherein we regard the other as if they were *part* of us, and therefore believe they ought to act like us. As we mature out of symbiosis, we need to embrace oneness, which allows us to see the other as a being *similar* to us, and therefore worthy of following their own path just like ourselves.

I believe that failure to grasp our oneness, while clinging to symbiosis, is the root of the whole world's divisiveness. Consequently, our hostility toward one another has long been aided and abetted by fallacious teachings about what makes for effective parenting. Children who ought to have been set free feel smothered, while children who desperately need to experience oneness with their parents feel abandoned. It's crucial to get the dance of separateness and togetherness right—at least as far as possible, since none of us gets it completely right.

Becoming attuned to our children's emerging capabilities doesn't mean relying on developmental charts or comparisons with their peers to tell us what our children can or can't handle, but paying close attention to how they are developing. This alone can tell us when we can pull back and let them take on more responsibility.

To make this concrete, let me tell you about Sally, an eight-year-old, and her mother Susie. Sally looked forward to playing with her friends every evening. But when it came time for her to go home and sit down to her homework, there were daily battles. Of course, her mother interpreted this as defiance. Only in therapy did she discover that Sally had a difficult time handling transitions. Her failure to adhere to her mother's rules wasn't coming from malice, but from a lack of skill when it came to handling transitions.

To address this, I suggested we use role-playing. Each time we got together, we took on a different role, practicing again and again how to transition from play to work. This repeated enactment facilitated dialogue about ways to help Sally transition more seamlessly. Following about four sessions, the skills we rehearsed carried over into real life.

In their natural state children enjoy just being themselves. They flow from feeling, responding to the as-is nature of life from moment to moment. Their natural state knows no compartmentalized categories of "compliance" or "defiance." All they are doing is *being*. It falls upon us as parents to help usher them into increasing independence and the responsibility that accompanies it, skillfully preparing and guiding them along the way, which is the nature of conscious parenting.

Chapter 17

Tricking Children
Is Tricky Business

Disguise it as we may, all child discipline is ultimately a form of manipulation—blackmail. You may recoil at the term "blackmail," but that's what it is: a way of coercing another to bend to our will. The onus is always on the child to change, rarely on the parent to understand the child in a quite different light.

Do any of us honestly believe that manipulating and coercing are healthy strategies? They are just forms of *tricking* our children, which amounts to deception. Over and over, research has demonstrated how detrimental manipulation and coercion are to a child's sense of self and wellbeing. Can lasting good truly come from tricking and bullying our children into conformity?

For this reason, I'm not interested in serving up strategies to elicit obedience. There are shelves of books in bookstores and libraries that enumerate all kinds of clever techniques to distract children, induce them to conform, and in some way manipulate them. All of these address the issue on a surface level. The focus is on controlling a child's behavior, pulling them in line; whereas it needs to be on understanding the child and thereby helping them become a person who is self-regulated, empowered, and autonomous.

You might argue that parents manipulate their children all the time. We manipulate them into going to school, doing homework, wearing warm clothes against their will, eating their vegetables, going to a place of worship, and a whole range of behavior that few children would naturally engage in. So what's the difference when we use discipline to manipulate behavior?

It's true that all of these are forms of manipulation to some degree—and the result in so many cases is that the child doesn't buy into what we are asking of them. Consequently, they dump the behavior at the first opportunity. Isn't this why so many children stop doing their homework in their teens? Children often lose interest in their hobbies and favorite subjects by the time they enter high school because adults and learning institutions have contaminated these innately joyous endeavors by imposing on them adult-like testing that isn't aimed at improving their depth of learning but focuses on grading them in comparison with others. Grades are a sport, the sport of schooling, and one everyone is forced to play. This is a sad situation we are all stuck with unless or until society as a whole, especially the educational system, changes—something that can happen if enough of us become aware of how manipulative the present setup is. In the meantime we need to work with the situation as it is as best we can, manipulating as little as possible and instead encouraging buy-in wherever this is feasible. To create buy-in means to allow the space for both dialogue and dissent. Many of us resist this as parents. Perhaps we tell ourselves we don't have time for dialogue, or maybe we don't even know how to engage on a level playing field.

When our children refuse to go to church, synagogue, or temple any longer, it's because this is another area in which they lose interest as they grow, no longer buying into what has often been forced on them by parents rather than coming from their own desire to explore ideas of faith. Thus one of the issues that religious institutions struggle with is the way that, when their young people go off to college, the institution loses them in droves.

Having said this, I want to make it clear that when I say the child needs to "buy into" a behavior, I don't mean we need to persuade them of its efficacy. Buy-in of a healthy kind is natural for a child, in that they adopt the particular behavior because it resonates with their own being. They connect with the behavior in a synchronous manner. For instance, do we have to persuade a child to play a game they love to play? Do we have to persuade a teenage girl to go out with her friends when this is one of her favorite activities? Do we need to yell at our children to eat something they find yummy?

Children are spontaneously drawn to activities that are synchronous with their being. This is why in kindergarten and first grade they tend to love going to school. Unless they are frightened by separation from their parents or some form of social dynamic, children at this age offer little resistance to learning. Why is this? At this age the teaching agenda is more likely to be aligned with the child's natural inquisitiveness. It can therefore be a joyous, playful experience for the child.

Manipulation tends to happen when a child hasn't bought into what we are asking of them. For example, eleven-year old Chris finally made it to the swim team, an achievement his parents were proud of. However, Chris was a reluctant team member. He hated getting up early in the morning for the swim meets and, even though he enjoyed swimming, loathed the pressure of the competitive nature of the swim meets.

Unlike Chris, his father Dave loved to compete and had been a competitor in the pool much of his life, which was his reason for wanting his son to excel in the sport. Since it was inconceivable to him that his son didn't wish to follow in his steps, he was constantly trying to motivate him either with threats or bribes—all ostensibly in Chris' best interest.

Chris knew just how to milk the situation, accumulating among other things the latest iPad and fifteen X-box games. To resist swimming was proving lucrative, which fostered his resistance. However, as his resistance increased, Dave began depriving his son of weekends with his friends, which stoked Chris' resentment. Compensating for the guilt he felt for punishing his son, Dave then rewarded him again, feeding a cycle that was growing increasingly dysfunctional. Perpetuating each other's misery, father and son were on a collision course.

Dave's parenting style isn't unusual. On the contrary, it's typical of the way many parents seek to motivate their children. It's a style that allows parents to believe they are sacrificing for their children. In Dave's case, were he to be told that his goal of seeing Chris succeed as a swimmer was driven by an idealized image of his son that has nothing to do with who Chris really is, it would come as a shock. The image he has of

Chris is a fantasy of his own creation, born of his own needs. In trying to shape his son in his own image, he was literally forfeiting a relationship with his real son.

This is perhaps one of the most common traps parents fall into. We are enamored with our image of who our children should be and how their lives ought to turn out—an image that has little, if any, connection to their true being. In contrast, to love our children for who they are in any given moment is to be fully present with their own self-propelled evolution, devoid of our incessant expectations. This requires us to discard any ideas we have for them and instead enter an awakened understanding of who they are—an understanding that needs to evolve as they evolve, requiring us to always see them as they are in the present moment, not as they were yesterday.

Had Dave taken this approach, he would have realized his son's naturally noncompetitive nature didn't gravitate to competition sport. This would have honored his son's feelings. Such simple acceptance alone might have reduced Chris' resistance to the swim meets. Instead, by forcing Chris to detach from his feelings, he triggered retaliation. The consequence was that both felt mad at each other.

It's important to realize that even the seemingly more benign tactics we use to get our children to comply with our wishes are manipulative. "If you aren't good, Santa won't bring you a Barbie," a mother tells her six-year-old daughter. "If you don't go to sleep in your own bed," a father threatens his four-year-old son, "you won't be able to watch cartoons." Or a parent may promise their ten-year-old, "If you get an A in biology, you can have the new bicycle you've been wanting." All of these approaches are manipulative.

As a result, we condition our children not to sleep, not to do well in school, and to have little sense of their purpose in life.

When we set up an artificial situation in this way, our children no longer do things because they are intrinsically the right thing to do. Bedtime becomes about watching cartoons—or, God forbid, fear of the boogeyman—not about the need for adequate sleep. Grades become about greed for the reward, not about learning because learning is naturally fascinating to children.

A child picks up on how important these things are to us. They realize we will do almost anything to get them to comply with what we want for them. By making these things so important to us, we undercut the child's instinct to flourish in their own unique way.

This naturally brings up one of the most common concerns parents have: How do we know when to push our children to do things and when to back off? Where's the line?

My daughter had been learning ballet for two years. Then her favorite teacher left, to be replaced by a stricter, more demanding teacher. After a few weeks I noticed that Maia had lost her enthusiasm for her classes. Dragging her feet, she made excuse after excuse to hang out at home a bit longer. When it became clear to me she was avoiding her lesson I asked, "Why do you no longer feel excited about ballet?"

"Because my teacher gives us scores," she complained, "and I got a two out of ten last time. I hate it. I don't want to do ballet anymore." After attending a few more classes, she refused to go. I found myself at a crossroads, pulled in two directions. Should I push her to keep attending in the name of not allowing her to quit simply because it was too demanding, or should I honor her decision? I knew how imperative it was that Maia felt heard and could take ownership of her own interests.

Initially I took no action but waited for the appropriate moment to have a heart-to-heart dialogue. "Maia, I hear your discomfort and your wish to stop ballet," I began. "I also know how good you are at it and that you enjoyed it with your last teacher. Perhaps you can change teachers?"

Maia was emphatic. "No, I don't want to do ballet anymore. That's that. Why can't you just accept it?"

"I can't because I don't want to encourage you to stop an activity the minute it becomes demanding. It's important to learn that not everything is easy, and sometimes we have to survive the tough spots."

As discussed earlier, so often we imagine our children won't be able to handle things, which causes us to go out of our way to protect them from the natural chaos, boundaries, and limitations that are an inevitable part of life. In this way we rob them of their resilience, thereby setting them up for failure since they lose touch with their inherent competence. However, we have to be able to discern when they are avoiding and when their heart isn't in something.

"I am not just giving up," Maia insisted. "I have done it for two years. It's not my thing. I don't just give up. See, I have been learning gymnastics and piano for three years. I really don't enjoy ballet anymore."

When I saw she meant what she was saying and that it was coming from the conviction of her spirit, I knew I had no choice. What *I* preferred for her was irrelevant. She was clearly communicating she was done. I knew it was more important for her to have a sense that her life was in her control, especially in the case of activities that aren't life-sustaining. I applauded her ability to know herself, affirming this was the most valuable gift she could give herself. In this way she was learning to trust her inner voice.

Although my controlling ego was triggered by this incident, I was able to set it aside and see my daughter's point of view. There was no need for arm-twisting. I didn't allow keeping Maia in ballet to become a personal crusade. For that matter, her being good or not so good at any sport or activity doesn't affect my sense of wellbeing. Besides, I truly empathized with her feelings of how her new teacher had turned something pleasurable into something competitive.

I was able to look Maia in the eyes and say, "I hear you completely. I see how in tune you are with your inner voice and that you aren't afraid to make a change based on what really matters to you. You also didn't just give up at the drop of a hat. You are making your own decisions, and I support you being in charge of your passions." This allowed Maia to realize her voice mattered. In this way, what could have been an unnecessary battle of wills now became an opportunity for connection and validation.

It's important to note that my decision to support Maia wasn't arbitrary but emerged from an engaged dialogue with her. There's no cookie-cutter approach to handling which optional activities our children should stick with and which they should allow to fall by the wayside. Children are entrusted to our care so we can help them discover their own unique being. Children know their heart—all we need to do is encourage them to follow it.

Chapter 18

What to Do When
Your Child Shuts You Out

"Sit down and talk to me. You never talk to me." Tanya's mother felt exasperated and isolated.

"What's the point?" Tanya retorted. "You never listen anyway. You don't understand a thing I say." Walking away disdainfully, Tanya rolled her eyes at her mother.

"Don't roll your eyes at me, young lady," the sixteen-year-old's mother yelled after her. "And don't you dare talk back to me!"

Tanya and her mother had reached a complete standoff, with the mother desperately trying to engage her daughter at the level of her surface behavior, which could only further exacerbate the rift between them. In my practice I see this kind of standoff all the time.

No one pushes our buttons more cleverly than our teens. I doubt there's a parent in this world who hasn't felt exasperated with their teen, clueless as to the best way to respond. On the one hand the parent wants to encourage a teen's autonomy. On the other hand the teen's seeming lack of respect hooks the parent into clamping down with even greater control. The parent is caught in a vicious cycle of desperately wanting a connection with their teen, yet acting in a way that pushes the teen away. As a result, both parent and teen suffer.

The teen years are perhaps the most traumatic for a parent, especially one who has until now gotten by on a model of control and dominance. For the parent who is used to getting their own way, having a child who now refuses to bend to their will can come as a shock. Many parents respond heavy handedly, which is the worst approach. Instead the parent needs to respond to their teen's need for both connection and autonomy based on their child's budding maturity.

In the case of Tanya, she may be acting in this manner for a variety of reasons, all of which are hidden from the mother's view. She could be indicating that she feels micromanaged by her mother and needs more autonomy, that her mother's wishes on an issue don't mesh with her wishes, or that her mother has no clue where she's coming from.

If a teenage girl calls her mother an idiot and the mother gets caught up in the surface level of the remark, she'll likely ground her daughter for "being so disrespectful," in this way cutting off all communication as the teen clams up. Instead the mother needs to recognize the term "idiot" has nothing to do with her intellectual capacity but is the daughter's way of communicating a message such as, "You just don't get me."

Instead of getting tangled up in the teen's language, the mother can recognize that teens use these words and therefore not make an issue of the terminology. She can also honor her own feelings by saying, "I feel hurt when you say something like this, and I would like to understand what it is you are really trying to say to me." The mother then needs to listen patiently and with continued detachment from the particular choice of words and actions, since her daughter may well talk back to her multiple times before she's finally able to voice what she's feeling.

Whenever we reprimand and discipline, we inevitably diminish honest communication, if not end it altogether. Then we wonder why our teens are so cold and distant. Ask any teenager why they don't talk to their parents and they'll tell you, "All they do is lecture me." In effect, they are saying that their parents are imposing their own agenda on the discussion, without truly listening to where the teen is coming from.

The objective of a creative dialogue around whatever behavior has emerged is to enable our children to meet their own needs within the container of the family's guidelines. The goal is always to empower the child to discover how to regulate his or her own emotions, which automatically results in behavior falling in line with the child's best interest. This requires us to create a safe space for our children to share their problems with us, so that we can creatively develop criteria that work for everyone involved. "Safe" means our child is permitted to say anything they wish to say without being judged, reprimanded, or punished.

I can't sufficiently stress that the reasons for a child's

> Whenever we reprimand and discipline, we inevitably diminish honest communication, if not end it altogether.

behavior may be entirely different from anything we have imagined. A clear demonstration of this is the case of Michael and his son Peter. Michael says to his son, "Do your homework before you get on the computer." Peter ignores his father and gets on the computer.

Michael maintains his cool but issues a warning: "I told you to do your homework; I won't tell you again." Peter continues to play on the computer.

Michael bursts into the room. "How dare you ignore me? If that's the way you want to play it, I forbid you to take your Pokemon cards to school tomorrow."

The next day Michael realizes Peter has taken the cards to school despite his express command. When Peter returns from school, Michael loses his cool, slaps the child, then grounds him.

In therapy with Peter, without the parents present, he reveals, "I'm having a hard time with my math homework, so I don't like to do it. I'm scared to tell my dad because he'll yell at me. And I had to take the Pokemon cards to school because all my friends bring theirs. If I don't have mine, they won't play with me."

Again, as we have been seeing all along, once we understand where the child is coming from, the need for discipline evaporates. The father punished his son because he feels helpless when it comes to getting his son to listen to him. It's this sense of helplessness that fueled the father's frustration and eventual anger. Had the father realized his son was behaving this way because of underlying emotional needs that weren't being met—feeling incompetent in math and wanting to fit in with his school friends—he would have handled the situation differently.

When I told the father what his son had shared with me, the father said, "I was so wrapped up in my need for him to be obedient, I had no idea what was really going on with him. Had I known, I would have understood his avoidance of math and helped him. And I would never have forbidden him to take his Pokemon cards to school."

Whenever we find ourselves repeating the same interactions with our children, it means what we're doing is ineffective. Were it effective, we wouldn't be repeating the cycle—the behavior would have changed. We refuse to believe our approach is incorrect, telling ourselves the child will "get it" if we just keep saying it often enough, loudly enough, or in enough different ways. Until we shift our focus to why our approach isn't working, the child's behavior continues—and we will continue to be mad at them. "Mad" in a literal sense, since going down the same road to the same disastrous end over and over is truly madness.

Going back to Michael and Peter, the father kept hurtling down the same track, getting the same results, never imagining his strategy might be fatally flawed. Had he become aware that Peter needed only one thing—to feel safe enough to express his true feelings to a father who really wanted to understand—none of these battles would have arisen. No discipline would have been needed.

When children don't feel safe to truly speak their mind, two dynamics are set in motion. One is that they bury their real feelings, since it's unacceptable and perhaps even unsafe to express what's really going on in them. The other is that they express their dissociation from their inner being by acting out. Because we haven't tuned into their feelings, they disregard ours. This is the root of the disconnect between so many children and their parents.

In how many homes does the parent, seeking to engage, ask their teen in the evening, "How was school today?"

The teen responds disinterestedly, "Fine. Can I go to the movies tonight?" There's a complete disconnect.

There are child psychologists and parenting books that will tell you it's normal for a teen to shut their parents out in this way—that it's a healthy part of their journey of becoming their own person. Nothing could be further from the truth.

Becoming our own person is entirely different from shutting someone out. Becoming our own person is the ability to be true to ourselves while also staying closely connected to others. At each stage of our development, we can be true to ourselves to the best of our ability and at the same time enjoy a meaningful bond. Becoming our own person promotes openness and sharing, not distance and a closed heart. Yes, there's a need for privacy as a child grows, together with the creation of separate relationships that may not involve the parents. This is healthy. But it doesn't mean a weakening of the bond with the parents and siblings.

Parents have traditionally been expected to know everything about their children. When a child is young, this is necessary. But there needs to be a gradual weaning as the parent increasingly trusts the child to pilot their own life. There's a gradient. If we honor this natural process, our children will want to share with us those aspects of their life that are appropriate to share. They won't resent us because they feel we are intruding on their privacy—or, on the other hand, that we aren't emotionally available to them and therefore aren't really interested in what matters to them.

I think of a girl of twelve who sat shaking in fear in front of me. Her mother and father had brought her to therapy because she had been hiding her grades from them, and they were concerned she was hiding even more things. The girl refused to share her reasons for hiding her grades in front of them, so I asked if they would allow me a few minutes alone with her. The moment the parents exited, there was a night and day difference in the girl's energy. She immediately relaxed her shoulders and wiped away her tears. "It's so difficult to tell my parents I'm scared of them," she confided. "They'd never understand. For them education comes ahead of my happiness. Nothing matters more to them than an A grade. Each time I do badly, they become so upset with me that I want to run away. I don't know what to do anymore."

I shared with the parents that the reason their daughter was shutting them out wasn't because she didn't want to confide in them, but because she didn't feel safe doing so. I explained that the teen years are a time in our children's lives when we as parents need to move from center stage to supporting cast. "This is a time for you to become your daughter's ally," I emphasized.

The mother balked: "I will never be her friend. I'm her *mother*." While the mother's sentiments lay in the right direction, in that she didn't want to blur the boundaries between parent and child, she was missing the essence of what I was saying. "Being an ally doesn't mean a blurring of boundaries in any way," I explained. "I'm not asking you to be your daughter's friend. By the same token, you are overly identified with your role as 'mother.' Because of this, your daughter feels stifled and made to feel like a child. Instead of being able to come to you trusting you'll respect what she wants to share with you, she hides from you like a toddler who has stolen a cookie she was told not to touch."

To this day, this mother has a hard time understanding how to shift out of her role as a parent. Because of this, her teen continues to act out in immature ways. The parent is still in a "doing to" mode rather than "doing with." The mother's inability to honor the increasing need for her daughter to develop autonomy, while still feeling connected to her parents, has simply escalated the teen's dysfunctional behavior. When children can't get their needs met in a healthy manner, they find ways to satisfy these needs somehow. Sadly the way they achieve this is often self-destructive, not to mention frequently resulting in havoc in the lives of those close to them.

Parents bemoan, "My kid turned into a monster the moment he became a teen." What they don't realize is that a monster isn't created overnight. The teen years can be explosive because, with the increasing freedom and ability to express themselves that come with these years, the child at last feels able to let out what's been building inside them for a very long time. Bear in mind that teens are told to grow up, yet they are very often treated like they were still five. For instance, in school, someone who is sixteen still needs to ask to be excused to go to the washroom! How grown up would *you* feel?

Such a child isn't a monster. The real monster is the accumulation of a mountain of unmet needs. The teen whose parent failed to tune into them as they were growing up finally decides that, since they are now older, they can take care of themselves. The problem is they don't know how to do so in a healthy way, so they pick friends and make choices that are harmful. For the parent who has no clue this is about unmet needs, these years can be a nightmare.

Dysfunctional behavior in our children is always about unmet needs. Even when children engage in deception and outright lying, the root is unmet needs. Such was the case with Justin. When his mother came to therapy, it was because she had reached her boiling point. Her son had stolen $200 from her purse, the latest in a string of increasingly negative incidents. Unable to cope with his disruptive attitude, she was ready to send him to boarding school.

Because I firmly believe every child wants to tell the truth if given the right conditions, I called Justin in to see me separately from his mother. As I predicted, from the outset he was able to open up. He confessed to his wrongdoing without hesitation, explaining that he used the money to hire a tutor for advanced chemistry because he was failing and was afraid his father, known for meting out severe punishment, would go berserk. The stark honesty of his admission was typical of what I experience with most children. "I know what I did was wrong," he told me. "I'm not an idiot. But having the dad I have, I live every day wanting to jump off a cliff. Maybe my mom is right that I'm a no-good loser. Perhaps it's better I go away."

The silence in the room was palpable. It wasn't the eyes of a thief I was looking into. I was peering at a boy who was desperate for approval and who had been pushed to underhanded ways by a family system that couldn't accommodate his needs.

I can't tell you how many young girls and boys I've met who have resorted to binging, starving themselves, stealing, overdosing, cutting themselves, lying, bullying, allowing themselves to be victimized, or acting out in some way or another in a desperate quest to meet an underlying emotional need.

All this trauma results from the fact that, as parents, we usually don't know how to parent differently from how we ourselves were parented. When our children awaken our pain from the way we were parented, all we know to do is to shut it down with control. Consequently our world is full of wounded, disempowered, dysfunctional children, who in turn become carriers of the tyranny to which they were subjected, passing it from generation to generation.

Although many of us are locked in conflict with our children much of the time as we seek to control them, we also simultaneously fear conflict since it awakens unpleasant memories from our own past. One of the ways this fear of conflict shows itself is how we tend to avoid defining boundaries and setting limits where they are needed. Not wanting to experience the discomfort of being seen as the "bad guy," we fail to say a flat "no" to our children when such is called for. The situation then escalates until the child becomes a tyrant, with such a grandiose and unrealistic sense of their power that they push us to the point of exploding at them— or their behavior becomes so aberrant, they create a situation that explodes in their face, wreaking havoc at home, at school, or in their social circle. By allowing our subconscious need to please to get in the way of providing the container every child needs, we do our children a great disservice.

Chapter 19

The Rule about Rules

"What rules should I establish for my child's behavior?" parents ask.

They are surprised by my answer: "The only rules you need are around safety. Those are the *only* rules I have in my household."

When I say that safety is a nonnegotiable aspect of a child's life, as parents we must be careful not to project our own fears into the situation, such as a fear of getting hit with a ball. To live is to risk to some degree. We need to make sure our own fears, likely rooted in our own childhood or what happened to someone else, don't stifle our child's adventure-some spirit. The courage to live adventurously is essential to a fulfilling life.

In the past I used to rely on an armory of rules like so many parents do. However, I found that I was becoming hooked on rules, imagining that the more I spelled out my expectations, the better behaved my child would be. By "better behaved," of course, we mean that we are more able to control our children. We don't realize that although we may achieve short-term control, eventually our children will resist and ultimately rebel.

Most of our conflicts with our children occur over aspects of life that are really quite trivial and not at all essential. We major in things that are minor, missing what really counts in a child's development. It's for this reason that I separate activities into two categories—those that are life-sustaining and those that are optional. I ask parents, "Do you really want to pick a battle over something that isn't life-sustaining and therefore isn't essential?"

By life-sustaining, I'm referring to activities like brushing teeth, bathing, learning to read and write, and developing social graces such as manners and being respectful of others. Such skills equip a child to cope with life's complexities. In these we ask our child to follow our lead, since it isn't merely our agenda—our personal preference—that's on the table, but something essential to their healthy development.

In contrast, it isn't essential that our child grows up to star on the swim team, be a scientist, drive a flashy car, or live in a fancy house. Once we are clear about this, fights about learning the piano or violin, taking ballet classes, or getting As all end. Sure, a good education can help certain children—although it's also true that many of the world's most financially successful people were hopeless at schoolwork. How many of us have gone back to school

> Most of our conflicts with our children occur over aspects of life that are really quite trivial and not at all essential. We major in things that are minor, missing what really counts in a child's development.

later in life and excelled because by this time we had a clear direction and interest in our chosen topic?

By not turning those aspects of life that are optional into issues, we allow a child's natural interests space to emerge, which is the key to their success. When parents take what's naturally life-sustaining and push it on their child for their own ego's gratification, they do the child a disservice because they have moved away from development and into manipulation. Now it becomes not just a matter of getting an essential education, but that the child must be at the top of their class and get into Yale or Harvard. It's no longer about running because your body enjoys exercise, but about becoming the equal of Usain Bolt. Instead of a matter of developing basic social skills, it's about fitting in with the chic squad at the country club. This is how we muddy the waters, causing our children to lose their way.

Life-sustaining activities are issues that are black or white. Activities that may be enriching but aren't life-sustaining enter the grey area. The parent can tailor activities to the preferences of the child, using these as opportunities to strengthen the child's sense that she or he is heard and valued.

Feeding children vegetables, despite their protests that they want fast food, is life-sustaining. However, we also need to respect the fact that peas may not be their thing; whereas broccoli they can tolerate. We can invite them incrementally to broaden their palate, but we shouldn't force a particular kind of food on a child who is repulsed by it, anymore than we would make ourselves swallow raw oysters or eat liver if such foods cause us to gag. We need to be aware that it isn't just about taste, either, but also the texture of foods. Science has shown that we don't all have identical taste buds or even the same number of taste buds. Some of us have far more taste buds, which means we detect texture in a way others don't. For this reason it's a mistake to insist we can all learn to enjoy the same foods.

Optional aspects of a child's development also include the particular hobbies to which our children are drawn, the friends they choose, and ultimately the career they select for themselves. In these areas our preferences don't count. Sadly many parents overstep their children's boundaries by interfering in their ability to make these decisions for themselves. Particularly when a child is young, this is done in the name of "exposing my child to a wide range of activities." When the child pushes back because the parent is so heavily invested in their piano lessons, dance classes, or other activities, battles ensue. Now discipline enters the equation as the parent seeks to impose their wishes on the child.

A parent may insist that for a child to succeed, the child must excel in the sciences. The parent's presumption that without science, the child can't do well, turns science into a life-sustaining activity in the parent's mind. Consequently, the parent imposes hours and hours of tuition on the child, thinking that science is essential to the child's future. For the child to drop it is unthinkable. However, the idea that science is life-sustaining has no reality other than in the parent's mind.

Religion is a more delicate issue, since many families regard it as life-sustaining. But is it really? If we believe our children should follow the religion in which we were raised, it will likely never occur to us they might benefit from being exposed to a variety of alternative views, including the possibility of not subscribing to a faith at all. I know of several cases in which children who chose a different path were ostracized by their families. I also know of gay individuals who are afraid to come out of the closet because of their parent's religious beliefs, as well as gay men and women who were thrown out of the home because their sexual orientation was considered "sinful." It's not my place to decide whether certain practices are indeed life-sustaining. But children need to be able to opt out of activities they view as non-life-sustaining, even if we think they are essential.

In place of rules, one can develop in their home a culture that all participate in. What do I mean by a "culture?" I'm referring to those things we all automatically do—activities that aren't optional. For example, in our family we all brush our teeth before bedtime. Since it's a life-sustaining activity, it's just expected that each of us will do this, and we require it of each other without any sense of guilt. We simply create a bedtime routine in which brushing teeth is one of the essential steps that's never missed.

When parents consistently engage in an activity like this, it becomes a natural part of the day. Taking a bath or shower, picking up our clothes and toys every time we finish using them, clearing the plates from the table after a meal to the degree that this is age-appropriate—all of these are life-sustaining activities we all do. In this sense, they are no longer "chores" that are assigned to a child, but just part of the running of the home.

A household culture in which all participate is so much more inviting than rules, which tend to connote a style of parenting in which the parent imposes a particular requirement on the child. I prefer to see parenting as a way of relating that emerges organically from the fabric of family life, avoiding a need for the parent to artificially impose a "rule."

In the same manner, a child's safety becomes a nonnegotiable aspect of family life, as the child observes the way in which the father and mother keep each other and each member of the family safe, such as by buckling the seat belts in the car regardless of whether the belt feels good.

Do you see why I no longer talk about rules at all now? I came to realize that the family's way of being falls into the quite natural categories of life-sustaining activities versus activities that may be enriching but not necessarily life-sustaining. By establishing a style of life—a family culture in which everyone participates—rules become unnecessary.

You can see why I moved away from the idea of rules if you think about how they go down with teens, with whom they are a frequent source of tension. If there's one thing teens hate, it's being told what to do. Having had to follow their parents and teachers all their life, teens now have an almost instant acid-reflux reaction to rules. And so they should! We as adults certainly protest when we are made to feel like someone's puppet, so why shouldn't our teens?

In the case of older children, parents need to realize the only thing that matters is the relationship we share with them. This is what's important at this stage. Rules go against a teen's budding

> I prefer to see parenting as a way of relating that emerges organically from the fabric of family life, avoiding a need for the parent to artificially impose a "rule."

independence, failing to take into account that the teen years are a time for increasing autonomy as the teen prepares to go out into the world. When parents impose rules, they are setting themselves up for conflicts they can't possibly win.

Our need for rules arises from our anxiety over our own ability to *lead* our children by example. Once we are clear about our own lives, so that we live with integrity, consistency, purpose, and direction, our own presence becomes our children's guiding light. Instead of imposing external control through rules, we rely on the power of our presence to guide our children, which is expressed in the connection we enjoy with them. In other words, we recognize that it's through osmosis that children learn best.

Chapter 20

How to Respond to a Teen Who Rebels

Many teens are alienated from their parents, in some cases dropping out of school, engaging in dangerous and even criminal behavior, joining gangs, or running away from home.

As parents, we often miss the signs that our teen is headed in a self-destructive direction, since we are so fixated on our own busy lives, concerns, and intentions for our child. Let's look at some of the common indicators that a serious rift between parent and child is occurring.

Teens often break curfew. When this happens, it's important that the parent doesn't take the attitude of, "This is rude, unacceptable behavior. He's being difficult, even defiant. I need to set him straight." Rather, the parent needs to recognize that the teen may have been doing something far too interesting to care about the rules. What's likely happening in the teen's mind is a subscript that runs along the lines of, "Your rules don't work for me anymore. I'm not a baby."

Another common reason for breaking curfew is that the

teen doesn't understand the value of the curfew and regards it as a means of control—and many times the teen is right. Parents often create rules that don't need to be created. For this reason, a parent is wise to reexamine the intent behind all rules, asking whether they are truly in the best interest of the teen's holistic development.

If a teen breaks curfew, a wise parent sits with the teen the next day—*not* that night, which is a time for welcoming them home safely—and opens the space for an honest dialogue about how best to satisfy the needs of both parties. Because it's so hard for parents to let go, they might say something like, "I need your help to see your point of view. Let's find common ground and discuss ways in which we can both get our concerns met."

I find when a parent approaches a teen in such a non-attacking way, the teen is more open to creating solutions that work for both parties. Perhaps the teen realizes that unless the parent phones them as curfew time approaches, they are likely to forget. The parent can then choose to phone the teen or maybe ask the teen to set an alarm on their phone for curfew time.

In some cases a teen stays away from home as a means of escaping a situation that's less than ideal. The parent needs to recognize how they contributed to a hostile environment

> **Parents often create rules that don't need to be created. For this reason, a parent is wise to reexamine the intent behind all rules, asking whether they are truly in the best interest of the teen's holistic development.**

for the child, taking the steps necessary to change things. In such a situation, it's crucial the parent is open for honest feedback. In this way any decision that comes out of the sharing is one the teen can truly buy into.

What if a teen continues to cut curfew even after honest dialogue? This is a sure sign the teen feels disconnected from the parent, which is why they turn a deaf ear to the parent's concerns. As one teen shared with me, "I don't respect my parents' viewpoint. I don't understand them. I don't feel they respect or understand me either."

In such a situation the parent is likely to conclude, "My child is going to ruin their life and I can't let them do this. They are heading for failure. I'm going to really show them who's boss." Now some kind of punishment follows as the parent's only recourse, further alienating the teen. Is it any wonder that in the United States alone, one in every seven children between the ages of ten and eighteen run away from home at some point, with between one and three million kids living on the streets at any given time?

What needs to happen is for the parent to hear the cry for help, which the teen has ratcheted up by ignoring things like curfews. The only kind of intervention that can work is that of sincere, concentrated dialogue, whereby each gets to examine their concerns and how these concerns are obstructing their ability to meet the other in the middle.

To accomplish this, it's often necessary to utilize the expertise of a skilled therapist. Only with such a professional moderator are the two warring parties at last able to see each other's point of view. Ultimately the parent will need to come to terms with how their approach has interfered with the establishment of consistent limits the teen can buy into.

What does a parent do if they find their teen is cutting class and smoking? From the teen's point of view, they are trying out new behavior as a way of asserting themselves. If they are honest, they really don't know what they are doing and feel quite confused. Cutting class and smoking can be a temporary relief for feeling lost, since both make the teen feel "cool." Such behavior begs for immediate help. The teen may well be saying, "Don't be afraid to come talk with me. Help me quit these destructive ways."

Of course, the parent who doesn't realize this is the message behind such behavior is likely to react, "How dare they do this to us? They are ruining our reputation in the community. They'll be expelled from school, and then they'll never get accepted to college." When such a reaction is followed by punishment such as grounding or loss of phone, television, and computer privileges, the child gets the message that the parent cares more about grades—not to mention how they look to other people—than about him or her.

The way forward is for the parent to reconnect with their child, helping them channel their frustration in a healthier way. Perhaps they begin to spend more time together at home. Perhaps they consider alternative schooling options to help their teen better integrate academic life into social and family life. Perhaps they go to therapy together.

Notice how in each of these scenarios the underlying subscript of a child's behavior is never what the parent imagines it to be. Notice also that the child's subscript is completely at odds with the parent's agenda, which results in a clash of wills. The child always operates out of a need, seeking restitution and reparation from the parent. Ironically, the parent also operates out of a need. The difference is that it isn't the child's job to fulfill the parent's needs—something the parent has to do for themselves. The parent's obligation to their children is to help them wade through their feelings.

Dysfunctional behavior is always a sign the child has lost touch with who she or he really is. This is why the idea of having rules isn't helpful. It's not about rules, but about connection—of the child to their own inner being and of the parent to the child.

If connection is important in the home, it's also vital if education is to be truly effective. Imagine if schools all sought to connect with children rather than focusing so much on rules. Sadly, many schools seem to be increasing the number of rules at the expense of authentic connection.

How can a parent of a completely alienated young person reconnect? A story broadcast on Mothers' Day, 2013, as part of the BBC program Songs of Praise points the way. The program featured a mother whose son became a member of one of the most notorious gangs in her neighborhood. Mimi Asher's first awareness of her son Michael's plight was when a police officer knocked on her door and asked to speak to him, explaining to her that Michael was part of organized crime.

Alarm bells went off in Mimi's head, and quite understandably, she plunged into a state of depression. Then she realized she needed to do something. But reaching out to Michael was difficult, since he wouldn't tell her anything. She realized the only route to him was through his friends.

Mimi emptied her living space of all furniture, creating a large open space in her home, replacing her comfortable chairs and other furnishings with snooker tables, television, and DVD equipment. Then she began inviting Michael's friends to the home as a place to relax and be themselves.

As the gang members began coming to the home, Mimi slowly began getting to know each of them, building a relationship with them. Eventually she became a mother to dozens of Michael's friends, washing their clothes, making sure she had food on the stove for them. "Everyone responds to love," Mimi says, "and love's the greatest thing of all."

No matter how hardened these young people were, they did respond to the love Mimi showed them. As a result, her son Michael transformed from gang member to a productive member of society.

Says Michael, "My mom was everyone's mother." It didn't matter that a lot of people in the neighborhood talked about Mimi for opening her house to so many young people in this way, questioning where her sense of dignity was. Says Michael, "People didn't understand the power of her opening herself up like this."

Mimi's intent to connect with the young people became the reason so many young people's lives were changed and her own son didn't end up in prison. As one former gang leader said of her, "I call her my second mother, and maybe about fifty others call her their second mother."

Whether it's your faith that opens you to truly love your child, your belief in the value of human life, or simply the fact you brought them into the world, connection in parenting is everything.

Chapter 21

Avoid Homework Battles

Audrey was having a hard time with her son Mike over the issue of homework. She constantly shared with me how they battled over his studies, which resulted in him saying things like, "I'm stupid, dumb, an idiot." Consequently Mike was now doing poorly in school.

I asked Audrey to videotape Mike's study sessions. When we viewed the videos together, they all began with Mike studying on his own. Then Audrey entered the room, standing behind her son and watching him. This caused him to tense up. Eventually, as his tension mounted, he bellowed, "What are you doing, Mom?"

"You're doing it all wrong," Audrey said. "That isn't the way to answer this question. You need to stop what you're doing and start over."

"What do you mean?" Mike reacted. "I spent the whole day at school doing this, and I only have a few more paragraphs left. I can't start again."

Audrey now resorted to scolding. "You're so lazy. You always want to take the easy way. Either start it again or you won't be allowed to go to the movies with your friends this Friday."

Mike slammed his book down on the table and stormed out of the room, yelling as he went, "I hate you. I hate school. I hate my life!"

The videos revealed that this had become a common scenario for Audrey and Mike. I explained to Audrey that although her intention was to help Mike do a better job on his homework, she was hindering the learning process because her interventions were damaging his self-confidence and eating away at his sense of pleasure in learning, thereby undercutting his motivation. "Why is it your job to play the role of his teacher?" I asked. "Did he ask you for help? Did his teacher ask you to help him?"

When Audrey admitted her interference was coming from her concern that her son wasn't doing well academically, I suggested, "If you take yourself out of the equation, Mike will adjust his effort to fit how he feels about what he has produced. Your presence is serving only to cripple his natural desire to do well, which is reflected in the fact he worked all day on a project you said he needed to start over."

Audrey got it, changing her approach from that day on. No longer needing to direct Mike's studies or show her approval or disapproval, she allowed Mike to self-assess and become self-directed. Within weeks Mike began regaining his confidence, engaging his studies with zest. He had become the pilot of his academic destiny.

Because there are many variables at play with academics, such as teacher-child relationships, peer pressure, a child's inherent academic ability, and attentional factors, a failure to study adequately is never a simple matter of defiance or laziness. For this reason, no one answer works for all children. It behooves the parent to ask questions in order to pinpoint where the child needs help. Let's look at how this can happen.

The parent sits with the child to talk about how best to help. In doing so, the parent is looking for answers to questions such as: What is my child missing? Why is my child resisting? What support can I offer? Does my child need extra help beyond what I can give? Is my child anxious about something? Can I model this for my child? Can I help my child orient themselves, while ensuring they don't become dependent on me? Can I undertake whatever may be needed patiently, consistently, and with compassion?

We tend to think we have to make our children study—that learning is something inflicted on children. It's precisely this kind of attitude that taints the learning process. Look at any small child who hasn't yet been conditioned to resist learning, and that child is naturally curious. A simple stroll down the sidewalk elicits a fascination with a worm or snail crawling across the path, a butterfly on a leaf, a bee collecting nectar from a flower. When we are preoccupied with our interests and fail to consider our child's interests, we don't allow time for our child's fascination with life to flourish. Traversing the sidewalk now becomes all about hurrying to school, ballet lesson, or the ballgame, not about the experience of walking in a world of wonder. In this way we kill our child's inherent love of exploring and learning.

Because our concerns are so often the only ones on our radar, our child has to fit our schedule, which conveys the message that the child's natural inquisitiveness about their environment isn't important. Then we wonder why, a few years down the line, we have to compel our children to learn, using manipulative strategies to outmaneuver the resistance *we* created in them.

Many parents complain to me that getting their teens to study is a nightmare. Emma is an example. When she was young, she was a bright, curious little girl who delighted in engaging with her world. When asked what she wanted to be when she grew up, she was always bursting with ideas. "I want to be an astronaut," she would enthuse, "or a police officer." Or she would talk about being a veterinarian, a gardener, a teacher—her imagination was limitless, reflective of her love of life. But by the time she reached middle school, Emma's confidence in her ability to be anything she wanted to be had been undermined by debilitating self-doubt. As a child she had said with a bright smile, "I'm smart, aren't I Daddy!" Now, at fourteen, because she couldn't make As in the way her parents and teachers expected of her, she resisted learning.

I want to emphasize yet again that when we fail to foster our children's natural curiosity, allowing them to develop in areas of life with which they connect instead of imposing a set curriculum on them that has more to do with our concerns than theirs, they lose their innate connection to life. Learning is no longer a delight but something imposed on them artificially. Is it any wonder they don't want to do their homework?

Our system of education often fails to focus on a child's natural inclination. In many cases, neither does it pay serious attention to the fact that, if our children are allowed to follow their own interior learning curve, they learn in different ways and at a different pace. One child may have an interest in math at age nine; whereas another has no interest in math at this age, then suddenly becomes interested in physics in high school, which naturally triggers a need to engage with math. As I pointed out earlier, when this student takes up math at the far later age of sixteen, it's with a completely different mindset. They absorb the equations more readily, perhaps even streaking far ahead of their classmates. This is because their interest is arising from an inner attachment to their chosen path instead of from a need to comply with a curriculum that bears no resemblance to who they are as a unique individual.

When we fail to foster our children's natural curiosity, allowing them to develop in areas of life with which they connect instead of imposing a set curriculum on them that has more to do with our concerns than theirs, they lose their innate connection to life.

A friend of mine was a good student until age twelve, when his interests took an entirely different turn. Throughout middle school and high school he dragged his feet, learning as little as necessary to get by. A student with the capacity to achieve academically, he was failing in school and was constantly berated by his teachers. Told he would amount to nothing and "end up flipping burgers for a living," he lapsed into several years of listlessness during which little other than television and rock music interested him. But in his mid twenties, now a short-order cook as predicted, he found he had a flare for cooking. After completing culinary school, he took an apprenticeship in a top restaurant, going on to open his own restaurant, which has become a roaring success.

A child who is failing a class may be doing so as a result of any number of factors, such as motivation, attention, and ability. Our task is to uncover which of these factors are at play, then create a program to help the child enhance their skills in these areas. When we punish, all we assuage is our own anxiety, while leaving the child with a sense of inadequacy and helplessness. In other words, discipline only exacerbates the existing problem.

How often do our children get punished for things they are simply unable to do? For example, a friend of mine grew up in England in the Baby Boomer era. If he couldn't multiply two numbers accurately, he was beaten. Why is being able to add, subtract, multiply, or divide a moral issue? Why does it require punishment? A child's sense that this is utterly unjust is bang on.

Because I believe that grades aren't an accurate indication of a person's intelligence and competence, I've never focused on them. They are simply a measure of whether you are good at the sport of schooling. But in all too many homes grades are a symbol of a child's worth. Effort and love of the process of learning are eclipsed by comparison charts and arbitrary scores. I feel so strongly that grades serve no meaningful purpose that I would abolish them altogether. For this reason, I don't pay attention to my daughter's grades.

Parents often ask me, "Then how do you teach your child that learning is important?" (Perhaps the question we need to be asking is, "How did our children unlearn what was natural for them?")

My response is that I encourage learning by focusing on her diligence in preparation for a test, while simultaneously telling her that once she has put in the effort, the test is irrelevant. When she comes home and asks, "Don't you want to know my grade?" I ask, "How did you feel about how you did?" I remind her that her own engagement with the material is all that matters, not what the teacher or her parents think. I actually don't look at her grades.

This doesn't mean I don't care about her teacher's feedback. But I focus less on her comparative standing in the class and more on her growth as a multifaceted individual, caring as much about feedback on her social skills as I do her math. I also recognize that her particular makeup will cause her to excel in some areas and do less well in others. And, of course, in no way do I believe that her grade reflects on me.

Taking myself out of the equation of my daughter and her engagement with her studies frees us both to focus on the skills she needs if she is to excel in life, without the pressure of pleasing her teachers or her parents. The result is that she has no test anxiety, which helps improve her performance. Too many of my young clients, even eight and nine-year-olds, are crippled with stomach cramps caused by acute anxiety about how well they are doing in school. Ask yourself why the suicide rate at top universities is so high. The number of suicides at Cornell has even led to the installation of fences on bridges.

The culture of competition is perpetuated by adults, not children, who simply enjoy engaging life in their individual ways when they are allowed to do so. We make everything about winning and losing. As one teen complained to me, "When I walk through the door after school, my mother never asks, 'How are you feeling? How was your day?' Instead she demands anxiously, 'How was the test? How did you do?'" This is how children learn that their performance is more important than their wellbeing.

What should a parent do if a child is faring badly at school? How should they react to the report card? Parents say to me, "Grades are a fact of life. Exams have to be passed. A child can't go anywhere without an education." Yes, these are realities that have to be negotiated. However, report cards are only a small indicator of how a child is faring academically, and certainly not a measure of a child's worth. From an early age, the parent needs to let their child know they don't put much stock in report cards.

Let me also add that the reason children resist homework is they resent having to sit at a desk again, having sat at a desk almost the whole day long. This is counter to a child's natural inclination and needs, especially for younger children. Homework is one of the most senseless inventions under the sun. When children ought to be out in the fresh air or engaged in something they enjoy, they are afflicted with additional drudgery after a day that's often been little but drudgery. Such is the insane world in which we live. If you want to add another level of ridiculousness, stress the need to study for a test. Is this really learning? Or is it simply a way of raising a child's anxiety, which will only lead to them forgetting what they studied as soon as the test is over?

Though our culture prizes a college degree, it's a simple fact that there are many college graduates looking for work. And, as mentioned earlier, many highly successful people never did well in school. Sir Winston Churchill, to name just one who played a critical role in preserving the freedom of the world, was forced to learn Latin and had not a whiff of interest in the subject. His grades were terrible.

Countless young people in their teens and twenties have no sense of purpose. Mired in apathy, they either avoid reality through self-sabotaging behavior, such as excessive drinking and drug use, or robotically go through the motions of everyday existence. The reality is they are lost souls who have endured so many years of being regulated by external manipulation that they don't know how to engage life from their deadened center. In the final analysis, the manipulation we think is going to motivate ends up killing the child's spirit.

Chapter 22

Why Do Children Bully?

How does a beautiful baby grow up to be a bully—or to abduct, rape, or shoot another human being? At the extreme, how does such an innocent infant become a sociopath or psychopath?

It's widely believed that serious dysfunction in a child occurs because the parent wasn't firm enough. Folk wisdom has it that they let their children run wild doing whatever they wanted instead of disciplining them.

I propose that it's often not discipline that's lacking, but a connection to the child's feelings that's been severed. Any disciplinary tactics the parent used only perpetuated the child's feeling of disconnection.

Lack of heart creates the bully, the criminal, the rapist, and the psychopath, not a lack of discipline.

When a parent or other significant adult in a child's life inadvertently sets up a situation in which they are so invested in their own agenda that they can't hear what their child is trying to communicate, the child grows up feeling invalidated. As a feeling of unworthiness wells up in the child, they are left with only two possible recourses. The first is to stuff their feelings down, which leads to anxiety, self-harm such as eating disorders or cutting, and in severe cases depression. The second is for the child to project onto others how badly they feel about themselves. Disempowered, they seek to disempower others. Treated like an object, they objectify others.

Lack of heart creates the bully, the criminal, the rapist, and the psychopath, not a lack of discipline.

I can't emphasize strongly enough that when a child's own voice has been either neglected or bullied into silence, the child can no longer respond to this voice, which is how they lose touch with the natural empathy of one human for another. Terrible things can then result, both for the individual and for those who cross their path.

Take the employee who is fired and goes back to their former place of employment to shoot not only the boss but several of their coworkers. This happens when a wound from childhood has festered for years. A situation arises that recreates similar dynamics to the individual's childhood, reopening the old wound with all the resentment, bitterness, and anger associated with it. These propel either the emotional meltdown of an enraged killer or the coldness that leads to a calculated, premeditated massacre such as happened at Sandy Hook Elementary.

I asked my daughter, "Have you ever been bullied?"

"Kids have tried," she said, "but I don't let them."

"What do you do when someone tries to bully you?" I asked.

"I walk away."

Why don't bullies come after her? Because the vibes she puts out don't invite engagement. Bullies sense her inner strength and realize they aren't going to be able to intimidate her. For instance, once when she was around six years old, someone told her that her hair was ugly, to which she spontaneously replied, "I happen to like my hair a lot, thank you very much." That ended the engagement.

A key element in preventing children from becoming victims of bullying is to encourage their assertiveness. Not aggression, but assertiveness—the two are fundamentally different. Parents encourage assertiveness when they allow their children's voice to be heard loudly and clearly in the family. A child who can be assertive at home automatically becomes assertive on the playground. Bullies can "smell" fear. A child who is confident has such an aura of presence about them that they aren't on the bully's radar for long.

This doesn't mean that even assertive individuals can't be viciously attacked at times. Strong, assertive adult women have been raped and even murdered, let alone children. However, while there may be an occasional incident—particularly if we are in the wrong place at the wrong time—it will be a one-off, not a pattern in a child's life.

How should parents respond to bullying?

There's no cookie-cutter answer. A parent has to gauge each situation, balancing the desire to swoop in and protect their child with the bystander stance whereby they allow the child to figure out their social relationships on their own. The response from the parent needs to fit the severity of the situation. All too often our children are being overprotected from the slightest social mishap, resulting in an inability to negotiate relationships on their own. However, it must be said that often parents err on the other end of the response spectrum, not paying heed to warning signs. For example, if a child is being cyber-bullied, screaming for help, it's the parent's obligation to jump in as a strong leader on their child's behalf.

To illustrate, a friend's daughter was the focus of vicious cyber bullying in which a website put out all kinds of slander about her. Refusing to allow her daughter to become a victim, the mother took action, going to the appropriate authorities to reveal the slanderous nature of the attack. The result was that the perpetrators were expelled.

In contrast, fifteen-year-old Amanda Todd in Vancouver, Canada, ended her life and left behind a chilling YouTube video in which she detailed how she had been bullied, blackmailed, and physically assaulted as a result of being pressured to bare her breasts on camera, then having the photo go viral. Amanda is seen in her video holding up a note that reads, "I have nobody. I need someone." This is where it's essential that parents and other caregivers are in close communication with their children, paying careful attention, reading the signs.

In Ireland, thirteen-year-old Erin Gallagher took her own life after enduring vicious online bullying, even warning on a popular social networking site that those who were persecuting her were driving her to hang herself. No one paid attention. In California, fifteen-year-old Audrie Pott hanged herself eight days after she was raped while passed out at a friend's house party—a pornographic scene that went viral as her alleged assailants, who were minors, disseminated photos of the assault online. Her parents knew nothing of the rape or persecution of their daughter until after her death.

In so many cases our children are screaming for our intervention, yet their pleas go unheard. When children aren't used to getting their needs met, they often don't have the skills to rally the support they need. Instead of demanding the help it's their right to receive, their voice is diminished to a whisper.

It's sometimes claimed that young people who fall prey to bullying and end up taking their own lives received a lot of intervention. This in itself is precisely what we are talking about in this book—intervention by parents and school personnel that's ineffective because it reflects the *adult's* agenda and doesn't truly connect with *the child's needs*.

Bullying is learned in the home. When we respond to a behavior such as hitting with the same kind of behavior, we send our children a lethal message: "It's okay to hit if you're an adult, but not okay if you are small and powerless." If a child hits, it's often because they feel disempowered in some way. Hitting them for hitting someone only serves to further disempower them, which in turn increases their need to defend themselves, leading to further hitting for self-protection and thereby creating a bully.

A parent needs to invest time and energy redirecting the child each time the child lashes out, teaching how to use other forms of communication. The manner in which we ourselves respond to frustration can help our child develop a repertoire of more helpful responses to their feeling of powerlessness.

Instead of disciplining children, which is inevitably directed toward compliance, parents need to teach their child to know their feelings and not be afraid to speak up if something isn't right. Coming to our children's aid when a situation becomes severe is important, but it's also essential we are attuned to their needs from a young age and teach them to be fearless when it comes to being their own advocates.

Again, the issue is that parents who are disconnected from their own true feelings and needs will fail to help their children, since they can't connect in the way their children require. Our disconnection manifests in the chasm between mind versus heart, doing versus being, ideology versus practice, institutionalized religion versus spirituality, and countless other ways.

The corporate world is also a manifestation of people's disconnection from their heart, where people believe manipulation is the path to getting what they want and therefore the way to succeed. People often use the excuse that "everyone does it." When a child learns at home that not everyone does it, things can start to change. The corporate world even celebrates the cutthroat approach of stepping over others, knifing them in the back, and scrambling to the top of the ladder at the expense of colleagues—behavior that reflects an inability to connect with and care for others.

Individuals like Bernie Madoff deliberately steal people's lifesavings because they objectify their victims. A gang rapes a beautiful young woman on a Delhi bus in India, beats her with an iron bar, and throws her to her death—and bystanders gawk, doing nothing, because they are disconnected and disempowered. Football players take advantage of a drunk girl in Ohio, raping her, because they have no sense of their own inherent value and therefore can't value

If we are to end bullying, all eyes need to turn to the parent-child relationship.

the girl. All of this is a failure of empathy rooted in the objectification that results from a child's feelings being trampled on and needs being unmet.

Wars, bullying, and religious infighting—all such expressions of hostility boil down to the illusion that there's a separation between ourselves and others. This results in our belief the other is against us. Quite naturally, we feel threatened and experience the need to attack back.

The sad truth is that every person who bullies or in some other way victimizes another human being is themselves a victim. Anyone who bullies another person was at some point made to feel bad, unacceptable. Such children dump their feelings of self-hatred on individuals they sense aren't going to fight back.

If we are to end bullying, all eyes need to turn to the parent-child relationship. Intervention programs at school can only touch the surface level of this complex problem, which has far deeper roots. Intervention needs to begin in the family at an early age, so that children learn to stand up for themselves. When a child is honored for the unique individuals they are, they feel no need to assert themselves in an unhealthy manner. It all comes down to each individual's right to exist as they inherently are, which creates the ambience in which they live their lives and from which they relate to others.

Chapter 23

The Challenge of Sibling Rivalry and Children Who Can't Get Along with Other Children

Akin to bullying in venues such as school, bullying also happens in the home between siblings. Sibling rivalry seems to be as ancient as human consciousness, stretching far back into our past as a species. The bedrock of Western culture, the Bible, even begins with a story of sibling rivalry that sets the tone for a lengthy epic in which brothers fall out—Adam and Eve's sons Cain and Abel, Abram and Lot, Isaac and Ishmael, Jacob and Esau, and others too numerous to mention.

How are parents to handle sibling rivalry? It depends on what's causing this rivalry—each situation is different. Behind sibling rivalry lies a desire to hook the parent's attention. At its root, sibling rivalry is rivalry for *parental* attention. Cooperation among siblings emerges when each child feels seen and validated by their parents. When one

At its root, sibling rivalry is rivalry for *parental* attention. Cooperation among siblings emerges when each child feels seen and validated by their parents.

child begins to feel the other is being favored, things go awry. However, when parents are able to instill within each child the sense that they will be treated fairly and with respect, children don't view each other as rivals, but as allies.

In a case I was involved in, Bob and Josh—two brothers three years apart—were getting into daily fights at home, attacking each other mercilessly. Bob, the older of the two, was cast as the "bad guy," since his parents thought he should have more sense than to hit his brother. In their minds he ought to be protecting his brother. However, no amount of reasoning, restriction, or even corporal punishment improved the situation. On the contrary, Bob's behavior grew worse.

When the parents came to me for help, I suggested that from now on, at least in therapy, they should encourage Bob to share all his feelings about Josh with them, no matter how ugly it got. I wanted them to see that the more Bob expressed himself to them, the less he would act out with Josh. For seven weeks I had only Bob and his parents come to therapy. In each session, I invited him to complain about his brother. We let him verbally assassinate Josh, slandering him without restriction, with me occasionally interjecting, "It sucks, huh?" or, "Wow, that sounds difficult." We never took his side or opposed him. The aim was to sit with his feelings, validating his perception of his reality. Once Bob began to feel he was being seen by his parents, and that he had their full attention, he began to let go of his rivalry toward his brother focus on what was going on within him.

At the seven-week mark something miraculous happened: the focus shifted from Josh to Bob's inner world, as he shared his fear that he wasn't good enough compared to his peers, wasn't smart, and didn't feel attractive to the girls. What had been masked as aggression toward his brother was now unmasked as the crippling low self-esteem he harbored. As his parents allowed him to express his feelings without qualification or restriction, he no longer had a need to be mad at his brother.

Bob had been cast as the "bad guy," though it was now apparent he was anything but inherently "bad." Really, judgments like "good" or "bad" are quite useless when it comes to parenting. To label someone in this way just means that a behavior either accords with our movie of how life should be or violates it. Such labeling only exacerbates problems like sibling rivalry. Instead, all behavior needs to be thought of as purposeful and examined for its meaning.

If a little boy is hitting his sister, the natural response of the parent is to say, "Bad. We don't hit." If the hitting continues, the child is then spanked or punished in some other way to teach him "not to hit." If the behavior still continues, pretty soon the parent starts to label one of their children as the "good" child and the other as the "bad" child, or at least the "difficult" one. "Why can't you be good like your sister?" the frustrated parent demands.

Whenever we see extreme behavior in our children such

as cruelty, it naturally triggers repulsion in us. If siblings are involved, we are automatically inclined to side with the child who is being victimized. The aggressive child then becomes cast as the abuser in our mind—and it can happen so subtly that we aren't even aware we have altered our energy toward this child. We begin treating the child differently, unwittingly judging them, withdrawing just a little of our affection, and thereby withholding the very connection they need even more than the other child. In other words, we unconsciously end up mirroring the hostility of the child right back to them, thus in our own way abusing them just as we have felt abused by them.

Labeling a child "difficult," "bad," "antisocial," or even "evil" serves no purpose other than to generate antipathy toward the child. Such labeling is disabling. Rather than critiquing the boy for hitting his sister, let alone labeling him, my approach is to look for the *message* in his hitting, because it's always there. It's crucial that parents know how to decipher what the hitting is really about.

This doesn't mean we allow the child to go on hitting his sister. On the contrary, we tell him to stop hitting—and, assuming he is small enough, if necessary we pick him up and hold him close to our body so he can't continue. By doing this, we foster connection instead of creating separation. Once we have established connection, we can then proceed to address the meaning of the hitting. Because children are essentially good, when we see a child hit, it ought to evoke in us an empathic response such as, "What pain they must be in to feel the need to hit."

This was the focus of a recent session with Andy and his four-year-old son James, who was repeatedly getting into trouble at school for hitting. Timeouts were a daily occurrence, followed by conferences with the parents. Still the hitting continued, to the point that Andy was at his wits' end. At home he had tried every reward and punishment in the book.

The first step for me was to connect with James, creating an atmosphere in which he felt safe and therefore free to express anything he wanted. As the therapy progressed, it emerged that he felt stupid and ugly around the other kids in his class. "They make fun of me," he confided. "They call me 'fatty' and say I'm funny looking." As a result, he was being left out of group activities and spent a lot of time playing alone. On the rare occasions when he engaged with the other children, his confusion over his unfair treatment was expressed by hitting.

Andy came to understand that his simplistic labeling of James' behavior as "bad" missed the point. Had he understood the purpose of the hitting, he would have seen the wisdom in his son's actions, realizing he was trying to communicate something vitally important to him. Had he had faith in his son, Andy would have known that James wouldn't be hitting other children unless there was something terribly wrong. Fear, not faith in James, had driven his reaction to the hitting.

As with Bob in the case I mentioned earlier, once we uncovered what was really happening in James, our focus shifted from his hitting to how he felt about himself. True, he was a little on the plump side, which invited taunting. Still, this wasn't the real issue. At the root of the other children's attitude toward him was a lack of confidence on James' part. Unable to muster an appropriate level of assertiveness in the form of his powerful presence, James resorted to hitting as a way of asserting himself. To hit was his way of feeling powerful. To express it in adult terms, he was saying in effect, "Don't brush me aside. I'm valid—I matter."

This may surprise you, but I now explained to Andy that his son's hitting wasn't "bad" behavior but "good." I then proceeded to redefine "good" and "bad" behavior according to the *intention* behind the behavior. Contrary to how we generally understand the term, good behavior isn't the conventional idea of what's "good," meaning compliant, obedient, and approved by others.

Good behavior is behavior that allows a child to feel present, self-expressive, and engaged with their own experiences. A child who cries authentically, laughs uncontrollably, dreams relentlessly, creates joyfully, speaks freely, and feels deeply is engaging in good behavior.

Good, then, is less about how the behavior looks on a normative level or compared with how others act. Instead, good behavior is behavior that's instrumental in allowing a child to be attuned to themselves.

If a child's behavior looks "good," such as achieving straight As and consistently being at the top of their class, but the child suffers from stomachaches, can't sleep soundly due to anxiety, or is constantly moody because of how hard they study, their behavior is in reality far from good. On the contrary, it's bad, since it deprives the child of a sense of their core completeness, ladening them with fear-based requirements, encumbering them with stress they don't need.

In other words, society has "good" and "bad" behavior exactly backward. Quite the opposite of the conventional view, a behavior is bad if it obscures the child's true self, leading to the adoption of a false persona. From this point of view, eye rolling isn't viewed as bad because it's "disrespectful." Instead of hooking the parent into disciplining the child, eye rolling should alert us to the possibility that our child is being forced to be phony. Eye rolling can be helpful if a parent is attuned to the child, since it reveals what's happening on the internal level.

When we move away from categorizing behavior and seek to understand it, we realize that far from anarchy, harmony is the result. Because children are free to be true to their essential self instead of conforming to our movie of how their life should be, their sense of their worth overflows in creativity. Because we trust them, they trust themselves and have the confidence to contribute from their internal richness. What a different world this would be if this were how all children felt about themselves. The turmoil that the disciplinary approach has resulted in for thousands of years would be greatly curtailed. Only if we see lack of goodness at the heart of reality do we tell ourselves that chaos would result if people were to follow the approach I'm advocating.

There can be other, hidden reasons a child can't get along even within the family. For instance, Mary and Jacob are great parents, yet they were struggling to handle their son's volatile, impulsive, tyrannical outbursts. Terrorizing his siblings, pitching daily fits, and getting into trouble at school, he was becoming unmanageable. Nothing they did seemed to work. Logical and patient by nature, they tried reasoning with him, explaining the consequences of his behavior, appealing to him in every way they could. Though they had done "all the right things" according to the parenting books, they were losing hope, not to mention entering a downward

spiral in which their son was full of resentment and manifesting not just anger but even outright hatred for them.

The situation only began to change when Mary and Jacob
realized that, despite their calm exterior, they were unconsciously tensing up around their son. Whenever they engaged
with him, their hackles rose and they became defensive.
Even though they clearly loved him, the very words they
used when talking about him belied the feelings he triggered
in them. You can hear this in how they described him to me:
"He's out of control. He's impossible. He does all of this on
purpose. We're disgusted and fed up." Even the best of parents find their energy drained in such situations.

These parents came to see that their son wasn't acting in a
deliberately vengeful manner. Rather, the executive function
of his brain—the part that involves the ability to manage
time, pay attention, change one's focus, organize and plan,
remember details, curb one's tongue and behavior, and so
on—appeared compromised in some way, resulting in his
inability to delay gratification and control his impulses.
This realization generated empathy on the part of Mary and
Jacob, opening a window for a different dialogue focused
on the kind of help their son needed and not on how dis-
tressed they were by his behavior.

What we see in the case of Mary and Jacob is a vicious
cycle in which the child increasingly embodies the unwel-
coming, even ostracizing energy of his parents and caregivers. Because of their ignorance that there was an issue on
the organic level, their child's behavior had become personal,
which led to perpetuating his antisocial tendencies instead
of providing the kind of intervention he was crying out for.
Often we don't realize how early in a child's life this cycle

begins. It happens unconsciously, setting up all the conditions that will eventually lead to the child's expulsion from school, becoming a drug addict, and even ending up a criminal, perhaps on death row.

How can parents identify symptoms of problematic behavior, look it squarely in the eye without denial, and take action early enough to avert a catastrophe—all without falling into the trap of labeling, and thereby beginning the ostracizing that leads to the social outcast who then may even gun down students and teachers at their school?

Parents need to understand that each child's neural network is wired differently and in some cases doesn't function adequately. The key is to pick up on this early, since these children need different kinds of social, emotional, and intellectual intervention than other children—and in many cases need carefully selected *professional* intervention.†

Symptoms of poor executive functioning include disorganization, emotional meltdowns over seemingly petty issues, and a desire to engage in risk-taking or dangerous behavior. Signs of these symptoms are often present in early childhood, though they can easily be missed by parents. However, as the workload at school increases, these symptoms flare up.

Children need help to handle these challenges in a preemptive manner. When symptoms are ignored or misunderstood, a child is often labeled and judged, leaving them with a low sense of worth. This leads to even more problematic behavior as time passes. Getting them help from early days can help compensate for the neural network issues, mitigating any deficits, and even leading to the brain rewiring itself in a more beneficial way.

† A list of resources is provided on page 250.

Chapter 24

When You Spare the Rod, You Don't Spoil Your Child

More than one parent has assured me that their child or one of their children is just plain "bad." Talking about feelings to help such a child connect with what's behind their emotional outbursts is futile, these parents tell me. Because the child is so "bad," the only thing that works, they claim, is strict discipline as a means of curtailing the child's nature.

There are children who do indeed have a hard time controlling their wild impulses, and some don't seem to connect to their feelings no matter what the parent does to encourage the child to become more centered. I explain to such parents that while I empathize with what they are experiencing, labeling their son or daughter as a "bad" child, then resorting to discipline, only escalates the situation, fueling the child's propensity to act out.

When children exhibit violence at a young age, even to the extent of torturing animals and launching vicious attacks on not only their siblings but even their parents, it's not surprising that some researchers insist there are children who are born into the world prone to defiance, rebellion, antisocial behavior, and potentially crime. However, I don't accept that some human beings are wired to go astray from conception. On the contrary, I've witnessed firsthand with many of my clients how discipline tends to be at the root of such behavior.

You can see this by looking at what sometimes happens to societies as a whole when strict discipline is used to raise their citizens. The macrocosm is simply a reflection of the microcosm, so that what occurs in the home is played out on a grand scale in national and international conflicts.

As an example of what I'm talking about, the Swiss psychologist Alice Miller in her brilliant study of the Third Reich entitled *For Your Own Good* shows how Hitler and his henchmen were the product of strict parental discipline. Research has also shown how extremely strict parenting lay behind the utter barbarism perpetrated during the ethnic cleansing carried out in Serbia and Croatia in the Yugoslavian wars of the 1990s. There's no question in my mind but that the disciplinary approach societies the world over have followed from time immemorial is a significant reason our world is such an unsafe and largely insane planet.

Even though we have seen how discipline can lead to toxic results, parents cling to the disciplinary approach and proclaim their pride in doing so. As an example, in February 2013, the British Justice Secretary stated in public that he spanked his own children when they were young, claiming that spanking children sometimes "sends a message." This government official also defended the right of parents to spank. This is in spite of abundant well-publicized research showing that spanking has long-term negative consequences.

Responding to the Justice Secretary's statement, a spokeswoman for the National Society for the Prevention of Cruelty to Children commented, "Whilst parents are currently allowed to smack their children, the evidence is continuing to build that it is ineffective and harmful to children."

Sadly, many households—and even many schools—all over the world still endorse paddling as a disciplinary tool. We refuse to correct our approach to our children despite the toxic results of such violence. This is largely because, despite all the advances in our understanding of our makeup as humans, billions on our planet still hold a belief that as a species we are prone to go astray unless we receive constant course corrections in the form of firm discipline. Thus for generations society has subscribed to the idea that if you "spare the rod" you will "spoil the child." Spanking and other forms of punishment are endorsed as good for a child because they are "corrective."

Some people justify this approach by attributing it to the Bible. Although "spare the rod and spoil the child" isn't found in the Bible, there are indeed statements like it. However, the precise wording of "spare the rod, spoil the child" originates from Samuel Butler in a poem entitled "Hudibras," dating back to 1662, the period of the English Civil War. The concept of sparing the rod and spoiling the child was also articulated a few centuries earlier by William Langland in 1377.

If we go to the Bible, particularly the book of Proverbs, we find statements such as, "Whoever spares the rod hates their children, but the one who loves their children is careful to discipline them."[1] In the New Testament, we also read that God "chastens those he loves."

---

1 Proverbs 13:24, New International Version.

If you really believe that spanking is effective, explain to me how our world has produced generations of dysfunction, resulting in massive personal pain, family members killing themselves or each other, mass shootings such as happened at Columbine and Sandy Hook, and even global conflicts such as World War II which resulted in the deaths of 50 million people. All of these situations were the result of societies that practiced "discipline."

It's important to understand that the "spare the rod" statements come from an archaic era when the human psyche was little understood. Those statements usually attributed to "wise King Solomon" about how a child needs to be beaten with a rod ought to give us cause for pause when we realize his son oppressed the people of his nation so severely that many of them finally revolted, splitting his kingdom in two. Just how "wise" Solomon really was as a parent should be judged by the results of his strict disciplinary approach. Clearly it backfired—as, in my clinical experience, does all discipline.

It isn't only cultures rooted in the Bible that believe in "spare the rod and spoil the child," but also most cultures with rigid hierarchies. Corporal punishment is readily meted out in many cultures based on a similar philosophy.

I want to emphasize that a child's behavior is always meaningful. Discovering the meaning of a behavior is the crucial task. If society would jettison the idea that some are inherently bad, we could begin to put in place social systems that might enable us to understand and help children who, for whatever reason, are struggling. Sadly, right now the help that's needed is largely unavailable.

As an example, following the massacre at Sandy Hook Elementary in Connecticut, several parents posted on

Facebook that their children were exhibiting the same behavior described by individuals who knew Adam Lanza, who did the shooting. While many judged these parents for depicting their children in this way, I respect their willingness to acknowledge the extremity of their child's behavior, together with the fact that, as parents, they are at their wits' end and have no clue how to cope with what's emerging before their very eyes. I especially admire those parents who can take responsibility by admitting, "Something I'm doing isn't right," as several of my clients have done. These parents recognize that the level of intervention their child needs exceeds the skills they possess as a parent.

Society as a whole needs to recognize there needs to be a culture shift so that asking for whatever level of help may be required isn't seen as a sign of weakness, which draws shame or an automatic call to the child protection services. The only recourse shouldn't be to take the child from the home, have the child arrested (thereby criminalizing him or her), or locking the child in a psychiatric ward. Various intermediary interventions are desperately needed.

We are talking about the large number of children who fall in the grey area, not those who need to be psychiatric patients or who have become criminal. One reason many parents of children who require help don't ask for it is because they sense that what's truly needed for those in this grey area isn't readily available. The support of mental wellbeing therefore needs to become a priority for society as a whole.

Another reason parents don't seek professional help is that family and friends tend to judge us if we talk about our limitations. As a culture we don't generally like to admit how challenging parenting is, and therefore we resist the idea of in-home assistance from a caregiver therapeutically trained to provide parents with a respite. At the community level, instead of treating each other judgmentally, we need to support each other in our failings and limitations.

When a woman posted an article entitled "I Am Adam Lanza's Mother" on Facebook, elucidating the struggles she was going through with her son, she wasn't saying she was literally Adam Lanza's mother. Rather she was trying to convey the feeling of helplessness she was experiencing because she couldn't get the intervention she needed for her son. In the end she believed she had no alternative other than to drop him at the police station. Many judged her, but the incident raises the question of safety nets for such a mother. Where does someone like her go for assistance?

One of my clients had a son who was twenty-four and was driving the family crazy with outbursts of aggression and threats of violence. His parents tried to obtain help for him, but because he was an adult their ability to do so was limited. The psychiatric wards released him within twenty-four hours because he could convince them he was "normal." When they called the police to their home, the police explained they couldn't do anything unless the parents wanted to press charges. Not wanting to do this, the parents felt helpless. This highlights how off-center our culture can be in terms of providing our children with the competent care they need.

As we discussed earlier, our educational systems are mostly about the head and not the heart. While on a surface level we talk about social behavior in schools, and in some schools counselors are available, school personnel are

We should ask ourselves, "Is it more important that my child learns algebra, or learns how to be fully present in each moment and to relate to their classmates in a supportive, caring manner?"

neither equipped in most cases nor encouraged to deal with what's going on in a child's psyche. But as New York Times science writer Daniel Goleman has shown in his landmark book *Emotional Intelligence*, a child's EQ (emotional quotient) is ultimately more important to their success than their IQ. Yet in most cases our entire focus, from the parent who wants their child to get good grades to the teachers and the curriculum, is related to IQ.

Schools could become a powerful adjunct to the home if we altered our focus from IQ to EQ. Instead of a curriculum that highlights weakness and fosters competitiveness, our children would be rigorously immersed in social and emotional training so that they learn how to regulate their feelings and express them in healthy ways. Other than learning basic skills such as language and general knowledge necessary to function in society, our children's day at school would focus on their overall development as a person rather than on the regurgitation of information—information that in the main can be learned rapidly in the future should the child need it in connection with a career.

We should ask ourselves, "Is it more important that my child learns algebra, or learns how to be fully present in each moment and to relate to their classmates in a supportive, caring manner?" I look for the day when the content of books like Eckhart Tolle's *A New Earth* and *The Power of Now* will be a major element of the school day, and when pupils will engage in emotional processing instead of mechanical testing. I also long to see parents of schoolchildren gather to discuss their struggles with their children on a regular basis, with a therapist trained in the principles outlined in my book *The Conscious Parent* present to oversee the discussion. This would go a long way to ending the senseless violence of our world—whether playground bullying, abuse in relationships, criminality, or international conflicts.

Chapter 25

The Hidden Reason
We Discipline

A child contravenes our wishes. We get upset. "Why can't they just do as they are told?" we ask ourselves. "Why do they always have to defy me?" Now we're likely to resort to disciplining the child to get them to fall in line.

On the surface, it certainly appears our children defy us. However, is this what's really going on?

When my daughter came down the stairs wearing one of her older dresses instead of the new one I bought her for the birthday party we were going to, I took it personally. In my mind, she knew that Mommy took the time to buy her a nice dress for the occasion. Why then didn't she just wear the dress I wanted her to wear? I was upset. She had done this to *me*.

In such a situation, we assume the child's desire for self-direction is a rebellious intention to do things differently from the way *we* want them done. If we simply asked nicely about their reasons, much of the time we would find them to be completely innocent and well thought out. But why can't it be that the child is simply expressing their wishes, which are equally as valid as ours?

When my daughter dressed differently from how I intended, it didn't occur to me that her choice of dress had nothing to do with me. In her mind she was simply wearing something she enjoyed and that matched her mood. *I wasn't even in the picture.* By inserting myself into this scene, I turned a benign action on my daughter's part into a battle of wills.

If we believe it's in a child's best interest to do what we wish them to do, we are likely to manipulate them into conforming. For instance, it's manipulation that's at play when a mother tells her daughter, "Mommy feels so happy when she hears you practicing your violin." Manipulation is also what causes a dad to say, "Son, you make me so proud when I see you out there on the football field."

When we manipulate our children in this way, we make them feel responsible for taking care of our feelings. Now it's no longer about their direct relationship with the party dress, violin, or football field, but about making mommy or daddy proud. If they become inclined to dress as they wish or to discontinue one of the activities we take pride in, they are conflicted. If they follow their own growth curve and it happens to clash with our wishes for them, they are likely to feel fearful of responding authentically. In addition, they may even feel guilty for making their parents sad. In this way their authentic self withers, which is why they turn to the kind of acting out characteristic of a false self.

Although our children's physical appearance is an altogether different matter from a party dress, many of us believe this too reflects on us. We want our children's appearance to be a feather in our cap. Often children are bullied because of their appearance, such as if they are on the heavier side. This can throw a parent whose identity is based on their child into a tailspin, causing them to hire a nutritionist, a personal trainer, and perhaps even resort to surgical procedures. Although not outwardly punitive, the underlying message such a parent delivers is severely judgmental. "You are not good enough," the child learns, "and need to be fixed. I will fix you." Such "fixing" is a form of discipline. "Fixing" a child because of image is fundamentally different from encouraging in our children healthy eating habits and appropriate exercise.

In the case of the birthday dress, where did the feeling I was being robbed of my power come from? It originated not with my daughter's actions, but with my own childhood. I was once the daughter who wanted to wear a dress of my choice but had to wear the dress my parents deemed more appropriate. Of course, the dress is just a symbol. At four it was a dress, at nine the piano exam they wanted me to take, and at nineteen my choice of boyfriend. This is how we end up replicating the way we were parented.

That we repeat patterns learned in childhood isn't the whole picture, for it doesn't explain why matters like our child's appearance, grades, acceptance into the cheerleaders or the football team, and other "marks of our success as a parent," stir up such strong emotion in us. Why are these such charged issues?

When I examined what was really driving my need to make my daughter conform to my wishes, I discovered it originated in an "empty" feeling that surfaced whenever she didn't comply. As the feeling persisted through the different stages of development Maia was going through, and the feeling didn't go away, I began asking myself, "What's this feeling about?"

It took me a while to see this, but I came to understand that whenever Maia challenged my image of myself as a certain kind of parent, I was exposed to the fact that *my own* authentic self had been crushed in childhood. It was the loss of access to my own true self that caused me to need my daughter to provide me with a substitute sense of self—an image of myself as a certain kind of parent.

It was quite an awakening to realize that whenever my agenda was threatened, I felt lost. Without my agenda, it was as though I was no one. The overwhelming emptiness I experienced triggered a level of anxiety in me that felt unbearable.

When we feel anxious but have no idea why we are anxious, one of the ways we cope with what we're feeling is to project it outward. When we do so, our children frequently become the recipients of our underlying fear. We fear for their wellbeing, fear for their safety, fear for their future; consequently, we discipline them to keep them under our "safe" control. Fear underpins much of how we interact with our children and is often the real reason we discipline them.

Of course, we justify our fear by telling ourselves we "love our children so much." I don't believe that to love someone means we need to fear for them. On the contrary, it's out of our fear for our *own* security and wellbeing that we fear for our children. We're afraid that unless the other behaves according to our movie, we will in some way be deprived of fulfillment or a sense of peace. This sense of lack, rooted in the empty feeling left by our crushed authentic self, gets confused with love. Unless we are able to discern the difference between love and our need for our children to assuage our feeling of lack, our connection with them will be muddied.

I trust it's clear by now that discipline essentially communicates, "How dare you make me feel inadequate? Because I'm now out of control, I'll show you who's really in control."

In other words, almost everyone believes parents punish their children for their misbehavior, and on the surface it would certainly appear this way. I'm saying that the real reason is different—so much so that I'm convinced we rarely if ever punish our children for their misbehavior. Instead we punish them for *making us feel inadequate*, causing us to become aware of what's lacking in our life—aware that our real self is somehow "missing."

The insight that discipline is really nothing but a crutch for parents who feel helpless when confronted by their own inadequacies is *nothing short of revolutionary.*

Once I realized that the way I related to my daughter as a disciplinarian started with the way my parents related to me, I naturally felt anger toward my parents. But I came to see that there's no blaming our parents for the crushed state of our real self, since they also had their authentic self crushed by parents who suffered the same fate, all the way back many generations. This is

> The insight that discipline is really nothing but a crutch for parents who feel helpless when confronted by their own inadequacies *is nothing short of revolutionary.*

why the world is in the sad state in which we find it, with so much hurt driving still more hurtful behavior—a state that has been perpetuated from time immemorial. Only now are we beginning to be aware of this vicious cycle that caused our grandparents and parents to manipulate us the way they did, and we in turn to manipulate our own children.

With the insight of what's really driving the urge to discipline, we can now begin to understand parenting in an entirely different light. Since discipline has to do with our own feelings of inadequacy, the main task of parenting is to address this inadequacy within ourselves as it's reflected back to us by our children. In other words, the focus of parenting isn't the *child,* but the *parent.* This means that becoming a parent is a wonderful opportunity to reawaken that which has been anesthetized in us by our upbringing.

When our children don't conform to our wishes and we therefore experience the pain of our own emptiness, the hollow feeling that results from having our true self crushed can only be filled by a renaissance of our own authentic being—a sense of who we are that, despite all the ways in which it was stunted by the way we were parented, is still present in us.

How does such a renaissance come about? Instead of lashing out at our child when we believe they are defying us, we instead sit with the feelings that arise in us at such a moment. The emotional discomfort we experience when we do so can be overwhelming, and the trick is to allow this pain simply to *be as it is.* We don't try to run from it, mask it with a busy schedule, or in any other way avoid it. We don't use our child to quench our inner longing. We just let the longing, the yearning, the emptiness exist for what it is.

Something quite remarkable now occurs. As we observe our emptiness, allowing ourselves to feel how painful it is, gradually we become aware that what feels like a bottomless pit is far from bottomless. Beneath the void and the pain it causes us is our crushed authentic self. If we go deep enough, we experience this authentic self, which begins to come alive, filling the void we feel whenever our children rob us of the self-image we derive from their looks, brilliance, accomplishments, ability to meet societal expectations, and so on.

The more we deal with our pain in this way instead of taking it out on our children by disciplining them to make them conform to our image of how they ought to be, the more of our children's authentic self we preserve and the less they will have to restore for themselves later. Thus parent and child become aids to each other's growth toward wholeness, with parenting functioning as a conscious partnership. Thus becoming a parent is the perfect setup for our growth, so we can complete for ourselves the growing up we weren't able to do as children.

What we are talking about is the symbiotic nature of the parent-child relationship. By this I mean that our children are initially part of us, during the womb and infancy, when we have to be intimately involved in all the minutiae of their lives, giving of ourselves at every level. But even as we become deeply invested, their wellbeing requires us to define a boundary between serving them and their needs versus using them to try to meet our own subconscious needs. Again, this is what I mean by our "subconscious agenda."

The fact we are caught up in the symbiotic "I am my child—my child is me" mode is why, when our child refuses to wear the party dress we bought for them, we take it personally. Or if they bring home a C grade, we act as if it's a reflection on *our* intelligence. In the case of the grade, instead of understanding the reason our child makes Cs in an emotionally neutral way, we guilt-trip or discipline the child to get them to make us look smarter. All discipline stems from the mistaken notion that the symbiosis necessary in the womb and infancy ought to continue unabated into the growing years and the teens—and, in the view of some parents, particularly in some cultures, even adulthood. Because our children need us in the early years, we become attached to being depended upon.

Infancy is often the hardest stage for parents to negotiate, while it's paradoxically also the most symbiotic. For the healthy development of a child, the early relationship *needs* to be symbiotic, so that parent and child form a deep attachment. Parents are asked to give everything of themselves, with one exception—their subconscious agenda, their own unfinished emotional development from their childhood.

This is why toddlerhood is a nightmare in many homes, as children assert their emerging independence. Why do we call this period the "terrible two's?" Because it threatens our attachment to the symbiosis. The toddler is screaming at us, "Let it go. Moving on." But since letting go of the symbiosis triggers in us the huge anxiety of not knowing our own authentic self, it's extremely painful for us to let go.

The same dynamic is at play when it's time for our children to go to college and we lay down conditions on where they should apply. Countless teens complain to me that they aren't "allowed" to apply to schools that are more than driving distance away—and since in many cases the parents

> It's crucial that we free our children of the burden of living out our dreams for them— dreams rooted in *our* needs, not theirs.

hold the purse strings, the manipulation works.

The goal of parenting is to love our child from an inner feeling of abundance, which means we don't approach them with fear for their well-being or success. Because we feel complete in ourselves, we have no need to make them conform to a need within ourselves. We meet our *own* needs from the authentic sense of ourselves we have begun to recover, which allows us to be there for our children in the way they require, free of neediness on our part. How they look or perform is no reflection on us. Wanting them to be happy and successful because *we* will feel better if they are falls by the wayside.

It's crucial that we free our children of the burden of living out our dreams for them—dreams rooted in *our* needs, not theirs. They then engage in the struggle of discovering their own voice and authentic path in conversation with the immediacy of their own experience, which is the best gift we can give any child.

Chapter 26

The Power of Connection

We need to connect with our children instead of imagining we constantly need to correct them. All children yearn for connection—*not* correction. They want nothing more than to feel loved for who they truly are in their authentic self. Not being appreciated for who they are is the root of all negative behavior, psychological problems, and social dysfunction, including criminality.

It's in the simplest of things that serious disconnection can occur. Our children instantly pick up our vibes and within milliseconds the tone for our interaction has been set.

For instance, a disconnect occurs in countless homes as a child gets off the school bus and enters the house. Before they have even removed their backpack, they are met with a barrage of questions: "How was your day? How did you do on your test? Did you enjoy your lunch?" Believing they are being a good parent by seeking to connect with their child, in the space of a

> All children yearn for connection— *not* correction.

few moments the parent has inadvertently imposed their own concerns on the child, directing the conversation according to where they want it to go.

Most likely the child isn't in a mood to report to the "boss." Exhausted from having to negotiate an adult agenda all day at school, the last thing the child wants to do is answer questions from yet another adult. All they need is for their mood to be honored.

Suppose the child was to say, "I don't want to talk right now. I'm too tired." The parent, wrapped up in their own movie and therefore disconnected from the child's feelings, takes this personally and, assuming the child is cutting them out of their day, emits a vibe of disappointment. However, the parent's feeling that they are being neglected is entirely a figment of their imagination, the result of placing *their* needs center stage instead of focusing on the child's needs. It's coming from the sense of emptiness that arises whenever their child doesn't function as a substitute for their crushed authentic self.

When our children are about to come home from school, we can prepare ourselves emotionally for their arrival. The key is to create a space in our agenda so the home is inviting to the child as they return from their day away from us. To achieve this, we allow them to set the tone. The only person doing the talking will be the child. I realize this is hard for many of us, driven as we are by our anxieties about our children, but this is how truly effective parenting is accomplished. Instead of disciplining our child, we discipline ourselves to keep our neediness in check.

When our child arrives, we open the door with a smile and receptive energy. Whether our child smiles back, hugs us, or even speaks to us needs to have no bearing on our receptivity. Whatever the child's mood is, the child needs to feel it's perfectly acceptable. In other words, the child is in the director role, asking for whatever they need from the parent to help them adjust to being back home.

As parents, we don't realize what a big transition arriving home is for our children. Even though we may want to ask about the test, the game, or any number of other aspects of the child's day, this isn't the time for it unless the child begins talking about these things. Without saying a word beyond a warm welcome, we follow the child's lead, allowing them to set the agenda. Once our child has replenished their energy and adapted to the home environment, we can then gently check in with them about their day. Most likely they will be open to talking at this point. But we don't push it. Rather we allow an authentic connection to unfold.

As parents, it's so easy for us to emphasize mental connection instead of emotional connection. This usually means talking. We think that by talking we are connecting, when we are often doing the opposite, imposing our wishes instead of listening to what our child needs. This is why the first rule of thumb is to silence our thoughts and enter into a state of utter stillness, which allows us to tune into our child's mood. This stillness invites our child to be whoever they perceive themselves to be.

How many of us can really enter this state of complete presence? To truly be with our children in whatever they are feeling can feel torturous to us until we become accustomed to it. We are so used to filling the silence with chatter. Our inability to simply be present with our children is one reason we develop all kinds of protocols for parenting.

No one teaches us how to enter into stillness. I mean, where is "stillness" on the school curriculum?

Being comfortable with stillness is part of the essential first step of a six-step method I recommend for establishing and maintaining connection with my child. To make these six steps easy to keep in mind, I use an acronym. The acronym is the word *winner*. The letters outline the method:

W – witness

I – investigate

N – neutrality

N – negotiate

E – empathize

R – resolve

Chapter 27

W Is for Witness

W stands for witnessing what's actually happening in the present moment. To be a witness to what's happening requires the ability to step out of the role of parent and into simply observing whatever is transpiring.

When you gaze at a magnificent sunset, do you gaze at it as a woman, a man, a parent, or a spouse? No, you aren't aware of any of these roles because the magnificence of the sunset has absorbed your awareness, so that you are fully one with the sunset. You have shifted from thought to presence, which enables you to become absorbed in the beauty of the moment. You are immersed in the "as is" of the event instead of interpreting it through the lens of a movie that says, "It should have been a brighter shade of orange." If your mind is full of mental chatter, you won't enter into the profoundness of what you are experiencing.

As you observe the sunset, you are still a woman, a man, a parent, or a spouse, but these roles are secondary to taking in what you are experiencing.

It's helpful to be aware that whatever is before us at a given moment—whatever is happening right now—contains a treasure if we can but recognize it, even if what's happening doesn't feel pleasant. If we are available and present, we may experience deep transformation; on the other hand, if our mind is busy we can miss these valuable lessons.

Can we connect with our children in the same way we connect with the magnificence of a sunset? Indeed we can, if we are willing to suspend our movie and encounter their reality as it actually is. Witnessing is about being able to connect with reality just as it is.

Many of us don't realize that when our children appear to shut us out, it's only because they sense we don't truly tune into them. "My parents never listen" is a complaint I hear all the time. Of course, we *think* we are listening. But what we are listening to is our own inner voices, not what our children are trying to tell us.

We wonder why our children turn a deaf ear to us. The reason is that our subconscious is constantly generating vibes that come across to them like a loud clanging. "All my parents do is preach to me," children tell me—especially teens. How else can a child protect themselves other than to turn a deaf ear to us?

Only when we are responsive to the moment instead of driven by our agenda can we meet our children where they need to be met. When we connect effectively, there's no drama. We deal with issues

> It's helpful to be aware that whatever is before us at a given moment—whatever is happening right now—contains a treasure if we can but recognize it, even if what's happening doesn't feel pleasant.

for what they are. This maintains the connection that's the foundation of a child's healthy development.

When a father complained to me, "My twelve-year-old never talks to me. He just wants to be on his computer chatting with his friends," I explained that this dynamic didn't appear overnight and wouldn't be changed overnight. I also explained that the son's behavior is a mirror of the way the young man feels his father behaves toward him. Because the son knows his agenda repeatedly gets trampled on, he's now communicating, "I will protect myself by going into my room, where I will take care of the things that matter to me for myself."

When I explained to the father that he needed to develop a connection to his son, he bemoaned, "But he won't even let me in his room. If he won't say a word to me, how am I supposed to connect?"

"You start from the 'as is' of the situation," I explained. "What does he do on his computer?"

"He studies and plays video games."

"Then this is how you connect—by showing an interest in a video game he really enjoys and inviting him to play with you." This is how you witness a child's reality.

"But I hate video games. They bore me."

"It's not about what excites you, but how to engage with your child. When he sees you are genuinely interested in interacting with him and not just looking for a way to change him, he'll begin to open up. But let me warn you, it will take time. You'll have to build trust one brick at a time. To do this, you can't let his rejection of you trigger you. See it as part of the process. It will help if you stay in touch with the fact he's only showing you how he has felt for many years."

Children aren't naturally closed off. On the contrary, they are open and willing to share themselves as long as it feels safe to do so. Children want us to see their inherent goodness, regardless of their external behavior at a particular moment. They delight in assurance their misbehavior won't faze us. To accept them unconditionally is what it means to witness our children.

When I speak of unconditional acceptance, parents sometimes say to me, "Aren't you telling the child it's okay for them to lie or steal or cheat?"

"This isn't about whether a particular behavior is okay," I explain. "It's about the *relationship* being okay. A child needs to be clear that it's safe to confess their mistakes and admit their weaknesses. It affirms for them that no matter what they do, they are still a good and valued person. Feeling good about themselves makes them want to do good things."

If our children smell a character assassination on the horizon, they clam up. There can be no judgment if we want them to open up to us. To enter into a state of witnessing means we forgo the urge to fiddle with the situation. Any adjustment of behavior has to come later in an atmosphere of meaningful connection. All that's asked for at this point is to witness their desire to be open with us.

When our children feel vibes of acceptance coming from us, they are drawn to spend more time in our presence—a fact we can see from the relationship between Fred and his daughter. Fred is a neat freak and loves to keep his house tidy. In one therapy session, he described a fight between himself and his daughter. "She's just so rude and disrespectful," he complained. It turned out his daughter had been watching her favorite TV show in the family room, when he walked in and found she had her feet up on the sofa, her books strewn all over, and was sipping a smoothie.

This was enough disorder to drive Fred crazy. "Get your feet off the sofa," he barked. "Tidy up your books. And take your smoothie to the kitchen. Don't you know that food isn't allowed in the family room?"

Fred's daughter got up with a humph, muttering under her breath, and banged her door as she stomped into her room. Outraged that his daughter had slammed the door, Fred barged into her room yelling, "How dare you! You are such a brat. I'll teach you. No more TV for a week."

When I told Fred that his energy had set the collapsing dominoes in motion, he looked bewildered. I explained, "The moment you entered the room, you perceived it to be in chaos. However, from your daughter's perspective, the room wasn't chaotic. She had set it up in exactly the way she was comfortable with. Her slamming the door on you was just her way of saying, 'I don't matter around here. Your rules are more important than my enjoyment.'"

Fred's mistake is to see himself in the role of fixer rather than simply being a witness.

Fred needs to learn to absorb the different ways of being of his family. Had he been a witnessing presence, he would have entered the room and, instead of homing in on the placement of his daughter's feet, her books, or her smoothie, felt the relaxed atmosphere and enjoyment she was experiencing. Had he allowed himself to feel this, he could have either sat down to enjoy the TV show with her or simply passed through the room with a "happy to see you enjoying yourself" smile on his face.

Thankfully Fred was open to learn that his critical attitude was really a way of avoiding intimacy and that his challenge was to address the subconscious fear he had of ever getting really close to another person. Through therapy, he came to understand that once he connected to his family in their as-is fashion and put the relationship with them before his agenda, he could then gently redirect them to help clean up where appropriate. In this way his family would be more receptive to his wishes without feeling as if this was all he cared about.

"I hear you, I see you, I accept you" is the powerful message of the witnessing state. This is the game-changer, the beginning of a new way of parenting that avoids battles over discipline and results in connection.

Entering the witnessing presence of stillness, openness, and receptivity can be a challenge. To help invoke a state of presence, I often suggest clients focus on the following:

> What lies before me is my teacher, I just haven't recognized it yet. What lies before me has been attracted by me to expand me in some way, and I will benefit from discovering how this can happen.

> What lies before me has come to me as a friend, not a foe.

> What lies before me is a reflection of my inner state, and how I react to it is a mirror of how I feel about myself.

> What lies before me is perfect in its imperfection— as, also, am I.

Chapter 28

I Is for Inquire

I stands for inquire. Let me state at the outset that this doesn't mean we pry into our children's lives like an investigator. I'm talking about getting to the underlying reason for what's happening. There are two aspects to this, neither of which involves launching an inquisition with our child.

The first aspect is to accept that we will never truly know another person, and neither is it our job to do so. The purpose of inquiring isn't to figure out who the person is, but to focus our energy on fostering a connection with them in whatever ways they wish to reveal themselves to us. This requires us to accept that our way of being is only one way of living as a human. There are infinite other possibilities, and it's each individual's right to express their unique approach to life even if it's entirely foreign to our way of being.

Because humans are such complex creatures, what we think we are seeing in a person's behavior is almost never what's really happening. Since we can't know what it is to be another person, we can only aspire to connect with them in such a way that the individual willingly chooses to reveal some of their internal world to us.

For another human to come into our life, especially into our care as in the case of a child, is a privilege. To be in their presence should fill us with wonder, so that we would never seek to control them. All we should ever want for this precious soul who has been entrusted to us is for them to investigate their own essence, coming to know what's truly meaningful to them, so they can blossom into the unique individuals they are.

Since we can't know what it is to be another person, we can only aspire to connect with them in such a way that the individual willingly chooses to reveal some of their internal world to us.

When we see the beauty in our children, their amazingly individual way of being, we are filled with reverence for them. All imperfection is understood in the light of a work in progress—a work initiated and sustained from within the child's own being. Our responsibility is to protect, nurture, and offer a reflection of the child's own essence, never to impose our way on them. Guidance is offered not to direct, but to allow the child to reflect on their own deepest desires so they might bring these to fruition.

The second aspect of inquiring is to discover the "why" behind a behavior—the why in *us*, the parents, not the child. What is it about *us* that led to the reaction we are getting from our child? What are we doing to spur them to veer from their own true being into aberrant behavior? Also, if the child needs some form of help, such as professional intervention, how best can we supply this help?

In my many years as a therapist, I've come to see there's always a good reason people do what they do. It may not be a reason that gels for us, or even one we condone. However, it's crucial we understand that in their eyes, their reason is valid. Especially with our children, it's important to get to the meaning behind any given behavior.

Often when we ask why someone does something, it's more of an accusation than a true investigation of reasons. There's no real desire to know the child, only a desire to change them. Unless we are truly curious, truly open, investigation goes nowhere. "Why" simply becomes a cover up for judgment and control.

Inquiry is about changing the focus from inquisitor to seeker—seeking to genuinely understand the dynamics. This softer energy invites our children to reveal themselves to us without feeling they are constantly coming up against our resistance.

An example of what I'm talking about is fourteen-year-old Marilyn and her mother Darlene, who had been coming for therapy to address a variety of typical parent-teen issues. Both felt hurt, trapped, and resentful of each other. On the table was the question of why Marilyn's grades had suddenly plummeted and she had become unmotivated at school. "Why is she failing like this?" her mother demanded. "How does she think she's going to be successful if she brings home a C in every subject? Why can't she see she's ruining her chances for a great life?"

I pointed out to Darlene that none of these questions were truly questions about the root of Marilyn's poor academic performance, when she had until now maintained excellent grades. The mother's questions were really saying, "For heaven's sake, why don't you stop watching those stupid shows on television all the time and start studying again like you used to." In other words, Darlene's "questions" weren't really questions at all but an expression of her utter frustration at her inability to fix the problem. There was no curiosity in the questions, no genuine desire to understand. As far as she could see, her daughter was deliberately messing up her life and needed to shape up.

"So what should I be asking?" Darlene said. We sat in silence for several moments. It was Darlene who broke the silence. "I'm really trying my best here," she said. "I thought I was showing my concern. I don't know any other way to say what I'm trying to say."

It was clear that Darlene had no clue there was an underlying reason for Marilyn's sudden lack of interest in school. It was also clear she had no idea how to connect with her daughter in such a way that Marilyn could feel safe expressing what she was experiencing. Nevertheless, there was a sufficient change in her tone to alter the atmosphere in the room. Marilyn could detect that the vibes her mother was putting out were those of genuine confusion.

I turned to the daughter and suggested, "Why don't you share with your mother what you are really feeling?"

Marilyn spoke directly to Darlene now. "You don't really care about what's going on with me, Mom. You never take the time to just sit with me and allow me to share things with you when I'm ready to. All you want to know is how my test went and what my grade is. You care more about having a smart daughter than about how I'm feeling."

Darlene's jaw dropped. "What do you mean, 'How you

are feeling?' I'm always asking how you are doing and whether there's anything you need, but you shut me out."

Marilyn looked at me helplessly.

Turning to Darlene I said, "Your daughter just shared something really important with you. In return, you said she shuts you out. Yet I just watched you shut her out. You rebutted what she said instead of hearing it. Would you like to try again, and this time seek to hear what she's saying to you?"

Darlene was stunned. For once she was at a loss for words, which became the catalyst for changing everything. Looking helplessly at her daughter, she mustered the courage to say, "I'm sorry I didn't hear you. Would you say it again? I really do want to know what's going on with you."

Marilyn teared up, unable to speak. At that point Darlene reached out to hold her daughter's hand, and for several moments they sat looking at each other in silence. Then, out of this stillness, Marilyn found the words to express what she had been going through, of which her mother had no awareness. It turned out it had begun with a boy who had made a pass at her but who was another girl's boyfriend. This had led to Marilyn's exclusion from a party to which all her friends were going. Feeling increasingly isolated and shunned at school, her interest in even being there had sunk to a low. The poor grades she was bringing home were a symptom of the emotional pain she was feeling.

Once Darlene understood what her daughter was going through and thought back to how important her own social life among her peers had been to her when she was a teen, she was able to connect with her daughter empathically. It was because her energy had shifted from critic to ally that her daughter felt safe sharing her struggle.

Earlier we talked about how parents attempt to assuage the feeling of emptiness they experience because their own needs weren't met as children. This was the case with Darlene. Whenever others sense this, they shy away from us. Because we're needy, our questions about them never feel truly curious but either superficial or accusative.

When our children sense we truly want to know what they are going through, they receive our questions as genuine opportunities for sharing. We can then gently guide them back to their own self-knowing, through which they are empowered to deal with whatever may be happening in their life, no matter how unpleasant it may be.

Chapter 29

N Is for Neutrality

N stands for neutrality. Because of our own emotional conditioning, we have a tendency to bring unnecessary emotion into any interaction with our children. For instance, if we want them to do something such as pick up their toys, hang their clothes in the closet, or carry their dishes into the kitchen, we have difficulty making our wishes known without lacing our request with emotion. The child, who always responds at the feeling level and not the level of logic, picks up on the emotion, which sets the tone for the interaction. If they hear a tinge of lack or anxiety on our part, it fuels resistance on their part, since they don't feel able to meet our need at an emotional level.

In the case of a request to put the dishes away, what's being conveyed to the child isn't a need for the dishes to be put away but the parent's need to be attended to. So instead of saying, "Put the dishes away, please," in a plain and straightforward way, there's often a slight panic or unwarranted intensity to our tone. When our request isn't heeded the first time, our panic rises in accord with our history of not being listened to as a child. Our voice is now louder, more pleading, as we sense we're losing control. If this doesn't bring the desired result, we experience outrage, causing us to yell, "What's wrong with you? Why don't you ever listen to me?" Our child looks at us in fear mixed with resentment, wondering what the big deal is.

When a parent comes from a state of wholeness, there's a natural strength to their request. If the child doesn't pick up on this powerful presence, the parent remains calm, positioning themselves in their child's view and making eye contact before asking firmly but kindly, "Is there some reason you can't fulfill my request? I need you to honor what I'm asking and put the dishes away." The parent then leaves the room with the full expectation their wishes will be followed.

Neutrality means we first deal with our emotional state, then ask for what we require free of all emotional baggage. The request carries no emotional overtones, such as "if you don't do this, I'll be so very disappointed," "shame on you," "can't you see how much I need your help," or any number of other subtexts that have no place in what should be a purely practical exchange.

Rarely do many of us ask for what we need in a matter-of-fact manner even the first time we make a request of our children, such as that they pick up their clothes. There's generally already a measure of emotion behind our request. It's this emotional charge that our children react to, setting in motion a dynamic that's counterproductive. Drama ensues.

It's one thing to remain neutral when dealing with a practical matter like chores, but what if you discover your thirteen-year-old daughter is having sex with her boyfriend?

Our first instinct in such a situation is to go ballistic and feel justified in doing so. In a situation like this, we bring out the big guns. We rationalize that our daughter's behavior warrants such a reaction. "How can *my* daughter have turned into one of 'those' children?" we ask ourselves. In our mind, she's going to end up a teen mom, a school dropout, a homeless bag lady. Surely this calls for a meltdown on our part?

It's understandable that we're inclined to go ballistic. Such extreme behavior on the part of our children evokes immense fear in us. The only way we know to react to such overwhelming fear is panic. How can you be "neutral" at a time like this if you care about your kid?

A young girl of thirteen who becomes sexually active, whether with multiple casual partners or with a boyfriend, may be manifesting a deep neediness. She is likely screaming for meaningful connection she hasn't found in her relationship with us and therefore lacks with her own inner being. Without an anchor, such a child forages for connection wherever they can find it. In such a situation, a boyfriend—or a string of casual relationships—provides a transfusion of selfhood. They are literally borrowing a sense of their worth, willing to pay any price. This is why a girl caught up in such a situation will even run drugs in exchange for the feeling of validity the connection gives her—a reality that renders imprisoning people for such behavior barbaric. What's needed is to help them develop emotionally.

Often we hear that a child who turns to such behavior has low self-esteem. This is a blanket term that tells us nothing. It even has a tinge of judgment to it, as if the girl ought to feel better about herself, valuing herself more highly. Terms like "slut" and "whore" are used of girls who become promiscuous as if they were making a conscious choice to sell their body. Even the term "unwed mother" is filled with derision and scorn, as if the girl had no sense.

When we realize that neediness underpins all acting out, and that emotional need easily overwhelms logic and good judgment, it becomes obvious that to go on the attack is the opposite of what's required. To become emotionally reactive only intensifies the guilt the child is already drowning in—not to mention that it drives the wedge between her and ourselves even deeper.

In such a crisis, what's asked of us as parents is to recognize the depth of the neediness our child is experiencing, then to intervene at this level. This needs to begin not with judgment, reprimands, or control, but with recognition that our own emotional energy has been a major contributor to the disconnection we are now facing.

> When we realize that neediness underpins all acting out, and that emotional need easily overwhelms logic and good judgment, it becomes obvious that to go on the attack is the opposite of what's required.

For parents to react at a time like this is to miss the point. The drama we create around the situation is merely a way of assuaging our own guilt and deflecting our anxiety onto our child. The horse has bolted, and it's far too late to lock the stable door with grounding, restrictions, withholding of privileges, and forbidding her to see her boyfriend or go out with her friends. Curfews won't change this situation. Restricting access to her boyfriend won't mitigate the severity of what's going on. No external approach to the situation will get to the root of the pain she's in. On the contrary, it will either drive the behavior underground or trigger an outright revolt, with the potential consequence of a child who leaves home and then really does land in dire trouble, perhaps ending up a prostitute on the streets, subject to the control of a pimp who affords her a tragically distorted sense of her value to him.

At such a time, it's essential that parents rein in their reactivity, which is the hardest thing for them to do when faced with such a crisis. They then need to realize that years of unmet needs can't be rectified with just one serious talk with their daughter or sending her to therapy.

Neutrality permits us to take meaningful action, which is fundamentally different in character from reacting. Neutrality removes the emotional weeds from a situation so we can clearly see how to move forward in a helpful way. When a situation is serious enough, I've often sent the parents and their child away for week-long intensive therapy retreats, where they immerse themselves in a healing process with their child under the guidance of a professional. Having said this, I want to emphasize that it's only a beginning. Years of feeling empty inside don't get filled in a single week.

While reestablishing their connection with their daughter over time, which will enable her to reestablish her connection with her own being so that she comes to truly value herself, it's important for parents to tolerate the presence of the boyfriend or other friends in their daughter's life. Part of their daughter's establishing of a solid sense of self is that she must take the lead in changing her behavior. The parental role isn't to dictate, but to connect. As a child's internal feeling of neediness begins to be replaced with a sense of their worth and competence, they begin to set higher standards for themselves, drawing to themselves situations and individuals who support the emergence of their potential. Only they can do this. Our role as parents is to provide a nurturing context for their flourishing.

The same principles I've outlined in the case of a young girl who is having sex far too early in life apply to children who are using drugs, engaging in other forms of risky behavior, or failing in school. The level of our intervention needs to be in proportion to the seriousness of the situation. A child who occasionally smokes a joint at sixteen is a very different situation from a thirteen-year-old flirting with cocaine, let alone addicted to heroin. At the core of all such behavior is neediness. The intervention needs to match the need.

When we get to the core of our children's issues, it's likely we'll encounter a lot of emotional pain. Often this will be expressed through anger, blame toward us, or sadness. These are weighty emotions for a parent to bear. Being neutral means being able to tolerate these emotions so we can help our children tolerate them. The more grounded we are, the better we'll be able to absorb our children's emotions. Slowly our children will learn to unburden themselves. In due course the inner impetus to act out will fade.

One client calls this "feeling work," referring to the process whereby the parent intentionally creates a space for the child to unburden their emotions. This client engaged in this process for six weeks on a daily basis. When her teen returned from school each afternoon, she allowed her to adjust to the home environment. Then she invited her to share her feelings. Because the teen was encountering social pressures and the politics of the playground, the mother knew it was important to be an equally strong presence in her daughter's life as were her peers. This required her to allow her daughter to unburden herself on a daily basis. Each afternoon they sat for about thirty minutes, writing, drawing, journaling, and discussing the girl's feelings. The mother listened patiently, allowing her daughter to accept that no solutions were needed, no outcome sought. Sharing was enough in itself. At the end of these weeks of intensive connection, the girl began to take steps to resolve her issues on her own.

The same principles apply in the case of a parent who finds marijuana, birth control pills, and a fake ID in their fourteen-year-old's room. To move forward productively, the parent tunes into their own feelings and recognizes the emotions this triggers within them. They may choose to connect with a friend or therapist to help them wade through their feelings, realizing that unless they process what they are feeling, they will create more chaos than healing.

Once they feel emotionally neutral, they enter a dialogue with their child. "I found these things in your room," they might begin. "At first I was shocked, but now I simply want to understand what's going on with you." When our children see our transparency and feel vibes that tell them we are truly calm and genuinely interested, they'll be more inclined to open up to us.

No matter how difficult it is to hear comments like "I hate you" or "it's all your fault," we need to remember that our emotional reactions only muddy the waters. Our children need to be able to unburden themselves without any judgment on our part. Emotional neutrality is what makes this possible.

Chapter 30

N Is for Negotiate

This second **N** stands for negotiate. The art of negotiation is one of the most valuable skills we can develop if we are to maneuver through the complexities of life in a manner that adds to us instead of detracting from us.

When we teach our children how to negotiate, we encourage them to see life as a creative process in which they are capable of influencing the outcome of situations. They discover that relationships can be mutually enriching, so that both parties claim their full rights as individuals.

We would all say we want our children to be empowered in this way. However, in practice we frequently undercut their ability to function from a place of power, which is what negotiation requires. How do we undercut them? By embodying the idiom "my way or the highway" as we resort to disciplining them.

Although the term "negotiation" is bantered around in the business world, I sense few really grasp what it means to negotiate. For many of us, especially in the corporate world, negotiation is a hostile endeavor in which there's a battle over who gets what and who gives up what. Winning is the goal, achieved at the expense of the other. There's no sense of mutuality, with both parties coming out of the negotiation as winners.

Is it any wonder that, instead of developing the skill of negotiation, our children learn to be oppositional, as if there were only your way or mine? They learn that the only way to get what they want is to go against us, hoping that by doing so they'll put sufficient pressure on us to cause us to cave into their wishes.

There are a variety of ways to approach life's many complex situations. For example, we can play a game with our children called A, B, C. We can use this game to illustrate there are always at least three different solutions to a problem—we just have to be open and flexible so we can find them. There can be way A, way B, or way C. If one party wants A, and the other party wants B, the way forward is to find C. Such a game instills in a child a sense of empowerment. They realize there's always a solution to a problem if we are willing to let go of our preconceived ideas. It isn't me versus you, but you and me together seeking fresh insight and thereby blazing new trails.

Many may view this process of negotiation as handing too much power to a child. However, the goal of parenting is to help children increasingly exercise power over their own lives, in line with their growing ability to manage such power. Besides, when you think about it, children are already powerful—and why shouldn't they be? Why are we so afraid of their strength? Coming from a place of insecurity and inadequacy, perhaps some of us prefer they stay less empowered so we can hold onto our false feeling of supremacy.

I think of Tyler, a boy who had a fit with his father in therapy. He wanted to get rid of all the tutors his father had arranged for him, especially pleading with his father to let him drop Spanish and English tutoring. As evidence he didn't need help, he pointed to his improving grades. In the negotiation that ensued, he agreed that if he could drop Spanish and English, he would continue to work with the other tutors. When I suggested this was a fair offer, his father retorted, "But then he'll think he runs the show."

I responded by asking, "Who ran the show in the first place by arranging for all these tutors?"

"I did," the father sheepishly admitted. "I wanted him to have the best chance possible of leading a successful life."

"Of course you did," I agreed. "However, although your son went along with the arrangement for a while, now he's asking you to meet him halfway. Such an agreement doesn't mean he runs the show. It means no one needs to run the show, but that everyone's needs can be met if there's respect and consideration."

It's important to be aware that negotiation revolves around those issues that aren't life sustaining. We don't negotiate on issues of safety and wellbeing. For example, if you are convinced by the evidence that sodas are detrimental to your child's wellbeing, you should have no hesitation in banning them from your house. If you need to take action in your parental role, don't be afraid to step into the leadership position and guide your child without a shred of ambivalence.

If an issue isn't life sustaining, children need to feel part of the dialogue. For example, one child wanted to go for play dates on both Saturday and Sunday, whereas the parent didn't think they should do both. When the child was resolute about wanting to go, the parent felt themselves slipping into the role of dictator. The inner dialogue began: "You are such a defiant, stubborn child. Sometimes you need to just give in to me because I'm your parent."

As the parent was gearing up to deliver a sermon, the child said, "I have a solution. If I finish my homework by Friday night like you want me to, I can then go on both play dates, can't I? It's only my homework you're worried about, right?" As the saying goes, "Out of the mouths of babes...."

Whereas compromise and sacrifice are based on giving up something important to us, negotiation is based on seeking win-win solutions. When we negotiate, we look for ways for both parties to get the best deal. We interact from strength, not by capitulating.

The parent instantly saw how, when challenged, she could have quickly shifted into her default mode of control. Thankfully, she chose not to go there. What did it matter to her how her child spent their Saturday and Sunday, as long as they had fulfilled the requirements for doing so? She realized the issue had nothing to do with the play dates, but everything to do with wanting things done in a way that made her comfortable. By not entering into a battle over control, she gained a far greater gift: an insight into how wise our children are if we only allow them to engage with us in a collaborative manner.

Whereas compromise and sacrifice are based on giving up

something important to us, negotiation is based on seeking win-win solutions. When we negotiate, we look for ways for both parties to get the best deal. We interact from strength, not by capitulating. The emphasis is on achieving something important to us. This is because the model is asset-based, not deficit-based. By this I mean that while compromise and sacrifice embody a sense of lack, negotiation rightly understood and practiced is grounded in an awareness of infinite possibility. We operate from the assumption that there's enough in the universe to make us all happy and we just have to figure out the way to manifest this. When we start from a feeling of infinite possibility, we quickly realize there are all kinds of options, plenty of choices.

To negotiate effectively, it's vital to be able to tolerate conflict. If we can't tolerate conflict, staying with it to a satisfactory resolution, we'll give up something important to us—and, ultimately, give up an aspect of ourselves. In such a situation, we aren't happy with the outcome, only happy to escape the anxiety that conflict evokes. The trick is to tolerate anxiety for the sake of maximum fulfillment, realizing that conflict is a natural part of engaging in any kind of relationship, especially close ones.

People often dread conflict, as if we aren't to have feelings that oppose those of the other. If you are an emotionally stable person, you should never disagree with another, right? Hence couples who want to present themselves before me in their best light despite having a child in deep dysfunction tell me, "We never argue or fight." They are surprised when I tell them I don't take this as an indicator of a healthy relationship. On the contrary, I explain, "I don't believe relationships that are conflict free are necessarily happier than ones that endure conflict. The key isn't whether a couple experiences conflict, but how they negotiate it. Conflict contains within it the seeds of real self-development."

Through negotiation, we learn to assert ourselves, while simultaneously learning to honor the wishes of another.

Through negotiation, we learn to assert ourselves, while simultaneously learning to honor the wishes of another.

Chapter 31

E Is for Empathize

E stands for empathize. Crystal's life had been marred with trauma and tragedy. Growing up in poverty in the projects, she had to witness the premature death of her brother in a drug feud. She learned early that she had to protect her feelings from the harsh realities of her life, encasing her emotions in a shell. As she never integrated the pain of her life, it lay festering like an open wound.

Intimate relationships were challenging for Crystal. Whenever a relationship threatened to go beyond surface impressions, deepening, she bolted. Finally, after a string of broken relationships, she came to me to seek an understanding of why she always closed up. "All my boyfriends think I'm cold and unfeeling," she explained. "They're scared of me and say I don't have a heart."

I explained how our past pain and struggles cause us to erect walls around our feelings so we feel protected. The pain is so great that we close off to deep feelings, which causes us to be afraid to get close to anyone again for fear of reawakening this pain. We tell ourselves we'll only be hurt again.

When trauma occurs particularly early in life, we especially shield ourselves from what we perceive as the emotional cruelty of others. One way we do this is to become cruel ourselves, since this kind of approach is all we know. However, let me add that when trauma occurs later in life, it sometimes has the opposite effect and opens us up to our heart.

As Crystal revisited her past in an atmosphere of acceptance, she began to reconnect with her buried feelings. Like a slowly blossoming flower, she opened up petal by petal, allowing tears to flow where before there had been only bitterness and resignation. Gradually returning to life, she found herself connecting with people as she never had—a direct reflection of her growing connection with her own deeper feelings. Her growing trust in her ability to handle pain allowed her to trust again.

When we are in touch with our own experience of being imperfect humans in an imperfect world and have learned to tolerate the anxiety this inevitably stirs up, we become open to others as they too struggle with the experience of being human. Having experienced similar pain, we understand them better. This doesn't mean we feel exactly what they are feeling or that we can presume to know how they are feeling. It means we are able to be present with people in what they are feeling, without thinking we have to fix things. We can simply allow each person to be wherever they find themselves.

People often ask me, "How will the other person know I care for them if I don't show them I worry about them, give them my opinion, or help take away their pain?"

I respond, "You are mistaking *doing* for caring. Empathy

is accompanied by respect for where people are on their life's journey. It understands that despite their pain, people are exactly where they need to be if they are to grow and become empowered. Our belief in their own ability to rise out of the ashes comes from our trust in the universe as a healing place that will usher us into a fuller life when we are ready."

Only to the degree we are emotionally connected with ourselves are we able to be present with another in their experience without the need to have it be anything other than what it is. It makes no difference whether we regard their issues as weighty or trivial. It isn't our place to judge what another is going through, since their makeup—and therefore what they can handle—is unique to them. All that's required is for us to be present with them in a wholly attuned manner.

To sit with another in their painful emotions is a challenge. Our instincts are to rescue the other from their pain. At times our anxiety may well up intolerably, causing us to jump into a situation unwarrantedly, thereby interfering with the individual's organic process.

To the untrained eye, rescuing might seem like empathy, but this is a mistaken view of empathy. To be in the presence of a person in pain inevitably triggers our own anxiety. The capacity to tolerate anxiety while staying fully

> Only to the degree we are emotionally connected with ourselves are we able to be present with another in their experience without the need to have it be anything other than what it is.

present with another's experience of the human struggle is what it means to show true empathy. To empathize with another, it's crucial we don't hijack their emotional experience and replace it with ours—a trap so many of us fall into. In such a situation, instead of manifesting a relatedness to their feelings, we contaminate the experience with our own unresolved issues.

When someone is in pain, we tend to offer a cliche such as, "God has a plan for you" or, "Don't worry, it will all work out." And then there's the classic, "Everything has a reason." These mean nothing to the person in agony, serving only to create a distance between them and us.

Most of the time what's required of us is simply to be attentively present with the person. When you feel a need to empathize, shift into a silent state, looking deeply into the person's eyes and tuning into their experience with your full attention. Just remain silent. If the other initiates discussion, the aim is always to direct the person back to their own knowing.

Inability to sit in the pain of life, whether that of our child or ourselves, shortchanges us, since only to the degree we can be with pain are we also able to experience the unbridled joy of life. In other words, it's our ability to experience the burning sting of our pain, without assuaging it, that empowers us to receive joy in all its magnificence.

We all want to raise caring children who, as adults, are able to engage in prosocial behavior and altruism. This begins with showing empathy to a child in all the little ways we engage with them at the youngest age. If our child breaks our favorite vase and we yell at them as if they had set the house on fire, we teach them to withdraw instead of to reach out to their world. They begin to come from lack instead of from a feeling of fullness. In this way we shrivel their capacity for altruism instead of expanding it.

Empathy is the opposite of discipline. Whereas empathy empowers us to tolerate both pain and joy, discipline cuts us off from our ability to go deeply into the experience of another with them. Because it involves manipulation and control, discipline will always limit the depth of our experience of life. In effect it erects a "road closed" barrier on the superhighway of life.

Chapter 32

R Is for Repeat, Rehearse, Resolve

R stands for, repeat, rehearse, resolve. Let us begin with the term "resolve," since the purpose of repeating and rehearsing is to resolve issues. "Resolve" has a double meaning: to resolve conflict, parents need resolve.

To resolve a conflict, coming to a state of completion with it, means the issue at hand is fully processed so that no niggling emotional remnants are left churning. This requires us to develop resolve, which then becomes a character trait our children learn to draw on in themselves.

I see many parents stuck in unresolved situations, mired in the complexity of problems, unable to find a way out. Being confused and stuck has become their default emotional state. Many of us are accustomed to feeling victimized by our situations and can't imagine feeling positive about our life. This negativity is emotionally cancerous and soon eats away at every good relationship in our life.

When clients come to me expressing that they have been at an impasse over an issue with their children for years, I first ask them whether they are ready to change their mindset. Naturally, they immediately imagine they need to do something dramatic to change the situation, so they are surprised to hear that the first step to change is nothing drastic, at least not on the external level. The first step is entirely internal, involving the individual's mindset.

I explain to clients who face unresolved dilemmas that every problem has only three possible solutions. We can change the situation, accept it, or leave it. If it's impossible to do one of these, then we need to choose from the remaining options.

How do we change a situation? We have talked about changing our inner landscape first. But then what? How do we help our children change their behavior? The most useful tools are repetition and rehearsal. As I mentioned earlier, I use role-playing with my clients. Through repetition and rehearsal, a child incorporates new behavior into their psyche. The repetition and rehearsal develop a sense of *mastery*.

Parents often ask me, "How often should we role-play?"

I always answer, "As long as it takes for the new behavior to settle in." If we want to create a new routine, it's going to take time. But the act of creating a new routine eventually instills a habit. This approach respects the fact that our children aren't being "bad," but are simply lacking a skill.

I use role-playing across the spectrum of daily life. It's especially helpful in transitional stages, such as first days at school, as well as when a child has a meltdown, and also in situations of conflict. Each family member takes on a different role, with each in turn enacting the various roles. As each of the family members feels what it's like to have the experience of the others, it fosters insight and empathy. When we have all experienced what it's like to be in the other's shoes, we brainstorm to discover solutions. These are then enacted also.

This approach isn't a quick fix. It takes patience, time, and often complex collaboration. Despite what parents say, I find few are willing to invest this level of energy to seek truly workable solutions. It takes a high degree of resourcefulness and resolve.

The hard part is that many of us don't want to have to choose a particular approach and stay with it, resolved to see it through. I tell parents, "If you aren't resolved to change the situation, doing whatever is required to accomplish this, then accept it. But you can't decide to embrace the status quo *and* be upset over the way things are. It's your choice to change things or accept them, and having made such a choice, resolve to be at peace with it."

Resourcefulness goes hand-in-hand with resolve, one feeding the other. The crucial thing is that, however we decide to approach a particular challenge, our children need to grow up in an atmosphere in which they are honored as vibrant spirits with a unique blueprint. In such an atmosphere, they learn to trust their inner voice, as well as to mine their inherent capacity for coping with the struggles of life. Because they are raised in an environment that guides them into their own knowing, embracing all their

The crucial thing is that, however we decide to approach a particular challenge, our children need to grow up in an atmosphere in which they are honored as vibrant spirits with a unique blueprint.

feelings—not just those that are "acceptable"—they are unafraid of feeling sad, lonely, or angry. Neither do they feel a need to shield themselves from experiences that might evoke such feelings. They then live with an openness that allows them to resolve difficulties as they arise, so they flourish as resourceful beings.

A sense of robust internal resolve equips a child not only for life's challenges but also for a lifetime of adventure. Having grown up with parents who are attuned to their inherent resilience, they are able to draw upon their strengths rather than becoming paralyzed by their limitations. Raised to understand that both their strengths and weaknesses together comprise the whole self, they don't feel a need to shun that which is less than perfect in them. In fact they intuit that this is precisely what makes them human and therefore able to relate.

While punitive approaches to bringing up children are widespread, overly sugary approaches to children are also in vogue today, which means I hear many parents telling their child, "Oh, you are so special." This is supposed to inspire the child, fueling self-esteem. In reality the opposite often happens. Children learn to have a false sense of themselves based on the *parent's* assurances, instead of an authentic sense of self grounded in their *own* competence. To tell a child they are "special" can give them a sense they are a cut above others, which carries with it the subtle message "and therefore you will be expected to perform better than others." This is fundamentally different from telling a child how dear they are to us just as they are, accepting them completely, and encouraging them to be true to the unique individual they are.

To say a child is "special" also risks fueling a sense of grandiosity, which is an inflated sense of ourselves and perhaps of our abilities. Although it's in vogue to tell a child, "You can be anything you want to be," it simply isn't true that every child can be absolutely anything they might wish to be. Not only is it not true, but the whole idea of specialness and the ability to be anything they might dream of being is antithetical to the complete and uncompromising acceptance of the child exactly as they are in their uniqueness as an individual—even if they don't stand out in any way and lead a quite ordinary life. Instead of communicating a blanket message to our children such as "you can be anything you want to be," it's more helpful to say, "If you are simply yourself, instead of copying another person or trying to be what someone else thinks you should be, you will find a way to express who you are in the world. By just being you, you will create a path for your life that's not only realistic, but that honors who you are." In this manner, we shift the focus to our children's inner communion with their deepest selves as opposed to a grandiose fantasy that isn't in alignment with their essence. This avoids problems such as young girls who fantasize becoming models, then often starve themselves to look like the models in magazines, despite not having the natural body type to be so.

It's crucial to realize that developing the resolve to live a fruitful life is something children do *themselves*, through their own self-discovery. It can't be artificially imposed, but rather is a natural byproduct of their gradual evolution when they are raised in an atmosphere in which the parent repeatedly guides them back to their own truth.

The worth of a child lies not in how others see the child,

It's crucial to realize that developing the resolve to live a fruitful life is something children do *themselves,* through their own self-discovery. It can't be artificially imposed, but rather is a natural byproduct of their gradual evolution when they are raised in an atmosphere in which the parent repeatedly guides them back to their own truth.

but in the child's own awareness of their uniqueness. None of this is related to the child's performance in school, on the playing field, or in the band. When a child's sense of self is measured by these external barometers, it isn't resolve that's being developed but fragility. Take away the external props and the child's sense of worth tends to collapse—and with it, their ability to function well.

When a young person develops resolve for themselves, they are positioned to explore their potential without holding back. In contrast, a young person who lacks resolve and goes out into the world to "become all they can be" is ultimately likely to collapse in on themselves—an experience we commonly refer to as "midlife crisis."

In other words, everything we've covered so far about allowing a child's life to develop on an authentic basis, not as a response to our cajoling and manipulating, prepares the young person entering into adulthood to construct their future on solid rock instead of on shifting sand. Not seeking to be what their parents want them to be, but resolved to be the unique individual they are, they build surely and securely, averting the typical midlife crisis that results from a lack of a solid identity. There's simply no false life to collapse around the person, and no unknown true self waiting to be discovered in the rubble.

By parenting in a non-disciplining way that fosters a child's own resolve, we are shooting for long-range development rather than short-term goals. We are allowing the orchard to grow and mature until it spontaneously produces a bumper crop of apples, rather than pegging apples on the branches of the growing apple trees so the orchard "looks" fruitful to the casual observer—until, that is, the apples rot and fall to the ground for the sham they are.

Afterword

Moving away from the idea of control and discipline is a challenge for most parents as it goes against all they have been taught and how they have been raised. This shift calls for a degree of awakening within the parent as they separate from their conditioning and move into a new way of functioning.

Along the way predictably there will be many setbacks as well as leaps forward. There are moments when we are able to flow with life in its "as is" state, fully aware of our feelings and connected to those of others. At such times we experience an inner spaciousness that allows us to stay present with the feelings of others without getting pulled into their drama. Yet it can take just one tiny misstep, one tiny occurrence in our environment, for us to veer off course. Suddenly our energy shifts and we enter an unconscious state.

This usually happens when something has triggered anxiety in us. Anxiety may arise because our sense of adequacy has been threatened or because our safety has been compromised. Children can be like gasoline and matches for unresolved conflicts in parents. Often these triggers occur in subtle ways, making them hard to identify. Needing our environment to be just so at such times, we resort to control. The members of our family immediately sense when we get like this and perhaps aren't shy to point it out. The issue is then whether we heed their input and take time to return to center. Of course, when we are in a state of inner disarray, it's hard to be open and accepting of feedback, especially when it runs contrary to what we want to hear. Yet it's precisely in these moments that we are given an opportunity to release our negative vibes and change course.

But how do we change course when we are raging? How do we muster such self-discipline?

It's undeniably hard to let go of our emotional reactions when we are in the thick of them. It involves abandoning the movie in our head that says things should happen a certain way. Given the time, energy, and money we have invested in a particular course, we are reluctant to change direction. Hence we rage at what's occurring, fighting to get things back on the track we think they should be on.

Even if we see the need to control our raging, we might tell ourselves that to back down will be seen as a sign of weakness. How can we simply retreat in the middle of a conflict?

Whenever we get into a fight, we set ourselves up for loss. In such moments, we aren't centered in ourselves and we aren't focused on the present moment. The question is: How long do we want to allow our past to rule our present life? How long do we want to battle with ghosts from another era?

Behind every parent's life story lies a child who was to some degree denied the development of their authentic self.

Our children deserve to be nurtured by parents who are journeying toward wholeness and discovering their worth, for it's from this that their own wholeness and sense of worth will be magnified. This is their right—and our calling in the sacred task of parenting.

Living out this life story, we now cheat our children out of their right to express themselves in their own unique way. Resorting to discipline to make them more like ourselves, we crush them as we were crushed.

Our children come with an innate wholeness and worth. They come to us with the hope we will nurture in them an awareness of this wholeness and worth. When we betray them because of our past conditioning, we deny them their basic right to be who they are.

Our children deserve to be nurtured by parents who are journeying toward wholeness and discovering their worth, for it's from this that their own wholeness and sense of worth will be magnified. This is their right—and our calling in the sacred task of parenting.

Tips for Staying Sane in the Conflict Zone

1. Don't Get Hooked

It's important to be able to recognize the ways in which our children trigger us. Is it their rudeness? Is it homework? Bedtime? The computer? In what areas do we face difficulties? Once we know what our triggers are, when we see ourselves becoming hooked, the first thing we need to do is *pause*. This is a time to step back, detach from the situation, and breathe until we are calm. This allows us to diffuse the situation for a few moments, giving us the space to catch ourselves so we avoid becoming unduly reactive.

2. It's Not Personal

Although our children are often at the center of our existence, we need to remember that we aren't the center of theirs. If anything, we are an onerous burden on them much of the time, obstructing their natural connection to the joy and fun of life when it's lived spontaneously. When our children express disrespect or anger toward us, we need to remember they are manifesting feelings that are more about their inner world, as opposed to about us. When we insert ourselves into the equation, allowing our emotions to be triggered, we lose perspective. Our ability to be of guidance and support to our children is then destroyed.

3. Time Yourself Out

Instead of sending your children out of the room for a timeout, try taking yourself out of the room. Go outside if need be or to your bedroom. Turn on the TV if necessary, but somehow distract yourself from your tendency to react. When you get out of the situation, you will begin to see things in a different light. If your child isn't listening to you, instead of begging, pleading, and cajoling, simply say, "I'm going to leave the room for a few moments." Say it calmly but firmly. By extricating yourself from a situation, you allow yourself and your child some much needed breathing room, which will allow you both to calm down. You can call a friend, write in a journal, take a walk, or read a book—anything to give you perspective.

4. Breathe

Learning to focus on the breath is a valuable tool to help calm the raging thoughts in our mind. There's no greater skill than bringing awareness to our breath. We simply sit in stillness and observe ourselves breathing in and out.

5. Pretend Everyone is Watching You

Whenever you are triggered and about to react, it might help to imagine you are in the middle of a crowded room with all eyes on you. How would you react if people you consider important were watching you? Would you scream and yell? When you imagine being in public, you create an awareness of how you might look to others, which can restore your sense of perspective.

6. Talk through the Feelings

One of the most helpful tools we have is our ability to communicate. Instead of acting mad, we can talk through our feelings. If we are insufficiently calm to be able to talk productively, we can state, "I'm feeling frustrated right now. It would be better for us to stop this conversation for the moment."

7. Make a Joke Out of It

Humor is one of the most effective strategies for allaying tension and altering the energy in a situation. We can sing, dance, turn a serious moment into a parody, or make a game out of it. Just be aware not to use sarcasm or discount the feelings of your child. Life is endlessly creative, beckoning us to be our most spontaneous and fun loving.

8. Use When—Then

Teach your child to develop solutions with you that work for both parties. Use the when-then principle. Let them know that their needs are important, just as yours are, and part of living harmoniously is finding ways to get each person's essential needs met. Think "both-and" rather than insisting on just one way.

9. Make a Choice to Change Things or Accept Them

Remember that you always have a choice in how you react to situations. If you aren't willing to carry through with whatever it takes to change a situation, don't blame your child for the way they are behaving. Instead, resolve to accept the situation and no longer make an issue of it. In this way you will at least change the dynamic in your relationship with your child.

10. We Are All One

Your child is just like you inside, with similar aspirations, ideals, frustrations, and needs. Instead of constantly projecting negative motives onto your child, step away and reframe your child's behavior in a positive light. In every behavior, your child is communicating something to you. What is it? Go to the need and try to meet it. This is where you build connection and create a sense of oneness with your child.

Clever Ways to Positively Reinforce Your Child without Discipline

Positive reinforcement is a way to teach our children their goals are achievable and praiseworthy. Positive reinforcement strategies serve as an addendum to the parenting journey.

The caveat is that such strategies must never replace the real foundation of the parenting process: the parent-child relationship. If parents rely on external motivators, children don't learn how to set and achieve their own goals. The ultimate aim of parenting is to encourage a child in self-initiation, self-motivation, and self-actualization.

Reinforcers need to be relational and experiential in nature. They can be used to help a child accomplish such things as studying for an exam, performing chores, improving their table manners, or stopping hitting. Here are 15 strategies I've found helpful with my clients:

1) JAR OF FUN: Place a jar in your child's room. In the jar, write down activities and experiences your child loves to do with you or their friends on separate slips of paper. Every week your child accomplishes a certain goal, they get to pick a slip of paper and enjoy that activity.

2) 360 FEEDBACK: Once a week, the entire family sits down and gives each other a 360 feedback on core contributions—chores, cooperation with others, goals accomplished, health, respect, and so on. Everyone writes one line about each other and about themselves. Then they discuss ways to help the person achieve their goals. This is a great way for families to share their feelings with each other, as well as a wonderful modeling tool for children to witness their parents being honest about their own limitations and their willingness to work on issues.

3) ROLE-PLAYING: Once a week, each family member thinks of one situation during the week that was either positive or negative. They enact the situation with either the people involved or another family member who takes on the role. The family then discusses what worked or didn't work in the situation, and why.

4) CHART CREATION: Every week, the children create their own charts for the week. They set out what they wish to accomplish for the week, describe how they will feel once they have done so, and decide how they would like to reward themselves. None of the rewards involve the parent buying something. The children can suggest games or activities the whole family can participate in as reinforcers. Having children create their own charts gives them the opportunity to organize their desires, while also stimulating them to find ways to achieve these desires on their own.

5) PICK THE MENU FOR THE NIGHT: Children who meet their goals are given the opportunity to select the menu for the night. This gets children involved in the planning and execution of the meal, while also giving them a chance to pay attention to the meal preferences of other family members.

6) BOX OF TREASURES: The parents fill a box with colorful pencils, erasers, and markers that the children can pick from once a week to reinforce the behaviors and tasks accomplished. Parents can make this a fun time for the children as they collect their "prize."

7) MOMENT OF SILENCE: Instead of punishing children for their negative behavior, the parent can use these opportunities to encourage quiet in their child's life. For example, if a child is rude or hitting someone, the parent can gently take the child aside and lead them into a moment of silence. Let them know that it's time to take a breather and enter stillness. The parent then sits with them to show them how it's done. After a minute or two, the child can be redirected into a conversation about the misbehavior, as well as praised and hugged for entering silence during a difficult emotion.

8) ALARM CLOCK FUN: Instead of playing police with your child, introduce the power of alarm clocks. Buy your child a few fun and easy-to-use alarm clocks and preset the alarms for the activities of the day: homework, bath time, reading time, sleep time. When the child finishes all the tasks at the right time, they can check off the day on a chart. At the end of the week they get a treat from the treasure box or jar of fun, depending on how many checks they collected.

9) VIDEO YOUR CHILD: This can be a tricky reinforcer and needs to be used with your child's consent. When your child is engaging in a positive behavior, you can video it. At the end of the week, create a collage of these movies to show the family. When a child sees themselves "on screen" engaging in positive behavior, it's more likely to motivate them to continue this behavior. It also allows the family to be involved in praising and motivating the child.

10) LET THE CHILD BE THE TEACHER: The best way to get children to learn a behavior is have them teach the behavior to someone else. Have your child be the teacher and let them instruct one of the parents in the behavior. Not only will this raise their self-esteem; it will also help embed the behavior with greater effectiveness than simply telling them what to do. Good examples of this are allowing the child to pick the activity for the evening and prepare for it in advance, with the whole family participating.

11) THE MANNERS PARTY: If your child is having a problem with manners, have a manners party. Pick out a few movies in which the people have impeccable manners and watch the snippets. Then practice for yourselves, and have a party while doing so. Get teacups, have tea and cookies, and pretend to have the best manners in the party.

12) CHALLENGE LADDER: Draw a ladder of challenges on a large sheet of paper and stick it on a wall. On each rung write down different gradients of a challenge. For example, if the ultimate goal is to read a difficult book, you might start with "reading two pages aloud with mommy." Then proceed to "reading two pages alone." Then proceed to "reading ten pages alone," and so on. This allows children to feel accomplished even when they aren't able to complete the big task at hand. It also teaches them that every big task can be broken down into smaller, more-achievable pieces. It's helpful for parents to have a similar chart in their room with a goal they are working on.

13) WHAT RISK DID I TAKE TODAY? Have a conversation around the table about the importance of taking risks and, more importantly, the importance of making mistakes. Teach your children that if they don't become comfortable with making mistakes, they will never take on new challenges. This exercise acts as a reinforcer for learning new behavior and challenging oneself. Have each family member go around the table and share their biggest faux pas of the day. It could be not exercising, messing up a piano practice, or being forgetful of someone's birthday. The bigger the mess up, the louder the applause. This teaches children to feel unashamed of their mistakes, and to own them without fear of reprimand or disapproval. Means by which we can improve can also be discussed.

14) DATE WITH MOMMY OR DADDY: This is a popular reinforcer. When the child has accomplished their goals, they get to choose a special activity with mommy or daddy, spending time alone with them. This serves the purpose of reinforcing the behavior, as well as strengthening the parent-child connection.

15) LOVE NOTES: Leave notes for your child in their lunch box or in random places such as their pencil case, on their bathroom mirror, or in their shoes. Be specific about exactly what behavior you are proud of and why. The more specific you are, the more meaningful the reinforcer will be. It's better to focus on process-oriented behaviors rather than outcome-oriented ones. For example, it's better to say, "I'm really proud that you spent ten extra minutes practicing that difficult piece on the cello. I saw how tired you were, but you still went the extra mile. That is pretty awesome of you."

My Child

My child isn't my easel to paint on
Nor my diamond to polish
My child isn't my trophy to share with the world
Nor my badge of honor
My child isn't an idea, an expectation, or a fantasy
Nor my reflection or legacy
My child isn't my puppet or a project
Nor my striving or desire

My child is here to fumble, stumble, try, and cry
Learn and mess up
Fail and try again
Listen to the beat of a drum faint to our adult ears
And dance to a song that revels in freedom

My task is to step aside
Stay in infinite possibility
Heal my own wounds
Fill my own bucket
And let my child fly

—Shefali Tsabary, PhD

Resources

If you have a child who appears to be struggling beyond the normal challenges of growing up, you may wish to explore the possibility of attaining professional help. There are several ways to go about this.

One is to call your health insurance carrier, who is in touch with a wide range of professionals whose focus is on specific areas of expertise.

If a child is of school age, you can also contact the school counselor, who will likely recommend appropriate neurological and psychological evaluation. Once an assessment of your child's strengths and limitations has been made, the assessor will make specific recommendations.

Two web resources may also be helpful:

The American Academy of Child and Adolescent Psychiatry: www.aacap.org

The following page will be particularly helpful: http://www.aacap.org/AACAP/Families_and_Youth/Facts_for_Families/Facts_for_Families_Pages/Where_To_Find_Help_For_Your_Child_25.aspx

The American Psychological Association: http://www.apa.org

Also by Shefali Tsabary, PhD

Written by Namaste Publishing author Shefali Tsabary, PhD, with the Preface by His Holiness the Dalai Lama and advance acclaim by authors Eckhart Tolle, Marianne Wiliamson, Marci Shimoff, Laura Berman Fortgang, and other leaders in the field of parenting, this book is a winner of the Gold Nautilus Book Award, Gold Mom's Choice Book Award, and Skipping Stones Book Award.

Dr. Tsabary's innovative parenting style recognizes the child's potential to spark a deep soul-searching, leading to transformation in parents. Instead of being merely the receiver of the parents' psychological and spiritual legacy, children function as ushers of the parents' development.

Once parents are learning alongside their children, power, control, and dominance become an archaic language. Instead, mutual kinship and spiritual partnership are the focus of the parent-child journey.

Parents unwittingly pass on an inheritance of psychological pain and emotional shallowness. To handle the behavior that results from this, traditional books on parenting abound with clever techniques for control and quick fixes for dysfunctionality.

In contrast, in Dr. Tsabary's conscious approach to parenting, children serve as mirrors of their parents' forgotten self.

The parent who is willing to look in the mirror has an opportunity to establish a relationship with their own inner state of wholeness.

Once a parent finds their way back to their essence, they enter into communion with their children. The pillars of the parental ego crumble as the parent awakens to the ability of their children to transport them into a state of presence.

Available at
www.namastepublishing.com

Our Service Territory Expands

Since introducing Eckhart Tolle to the world with *The Power of Now* in 1997 (followed by *Stillness Speaks, A New Earth,* and *Milton's Secret*), NAMASTE PUBLISHING has been committed to bringing forward only the most evolutionary and transformational publications that acknowledge and encourage us to awaken to who we truly are: spiritual beings of inestimable value and creative power.

In our commitment to expand our service purpose—indeed, to redefine it— we have created a unique website that provides a global spiritual gathering place to support and nurture individual and collective evolution in consciousness. You will have access to our publications in a variety of formats: traditional books, eBooks, audiobooks, CDs, and DVDs. Increasingly, our publications are available for instant download.

We invite you to get to know our authors by going to their individual pages on the website. We also invite you to read our blogs: The Compassionate Eye, Consciousness Rising, Conscious Parenting, and Health. Enjoy the wisdom of Bizah, a lovable student of Zen, presented in daily and weekly entries.

We are each in our different ways both teachers and students. For this reason, the Namaste spiritual community provides an opportunity to meet other members of the community, share your insights, update your "spiritual status," and contribute to our online spiritual dictionary.

We also invite you to sign up for our free ezine *Namaste Insights*, which is packed with cutting edge articles on spirituality, many of them written by leading spiritual teachers. The ezine is only available electronically and is not produced on a set schedule.

What better way to experience the reality and benefits of our oneness than by gathering in spiritual community? Tap into the power of collective consciousness and help us bring about a more loving world.

We request the honor of your presence at
www.namastepublishing.com